VEDANTA PHILOSOPHY

INSPIRED TALKS

VEDANTA PHILOSOPHY

INSPIRED TALKS

SWAMI VIVEKANANDA

GYAN

Published by

GYAN

Gyan Publishing House
5, Ansari Road
Daryaganj, New Delhi-110002
Phone: 011-47034999, 9811692060
E-mail: books@gyanbooks.com

Distribution Network
gyanbooks.com
India, USA, Canada, UK, Australia, France

ISBN: 978-81-212-8660-2 (PB)
First Published, 1908

2nd Impression 2023

Printed at: Gyan Press, Delhi.

VEDANTA PHILOSOPHY INSPIRED TALKS
Author: Swami Vivekananda

SWAMI VIVEKANANDA

(From a photograph taken just before leaving Madras for the Parliament of Religions at Chicago, showing the Swami in the orange robe and with the shaven head of the Sanyasin.)

VEDANTA PHILOSOPHY

INSPIRED TALKS

BY

SWAMI VIVEKANANDA

(Recorded by a disciple during the seven weeks at Thousand Island Park)

Second Edition

PUBLISHED BY
THE RAMAKRISHNA MISSION
MYLAPORE, MADRAS

To His Holiness
SWAMI BRAHMANANDAJI
In Loving Memory
OF
SWAMI VIVEKANANDA
This Book
IS DEDICATED BY
His Devoted Disciples.

INSPIRED TALKS

CONTENTS

HOUSE WHERE SWAMI VIVEKANANDA LIVED AT THOUSAND ISLAND PARK

(The upper open window in the left-hand wing belonged to the Swami's room. The upper piazza was where the evening talks were given and the Swami's seat was at the end near his room.)

PREFACE

This invaluable book is published for the second time. In this edition I have added a few notes where Swamiji's utterances may appear to be abrupt and unconnected. Some typographical mistakes also have been attended to and no pains have been spared to make it intelligible to all readers and free from all errors, as far as possible.

Swamiji is known all over the world as the greatest and most powerful exponent of the Vedânta in modern times. Many have felt the irresistible charm of his eloquence in India and abroad. In the present case Swamiji did not stand before a vast and critical audience to conquer them by his irrefutable arguments based upon sound logic, his bewitching personality and his rare gifts of explaining the most abstruse subjects in a most perspicuous manner accompanied by his "cyclonic" eloquence, but he was sitting before a few of his already conquered chosen disciples who had begun to see in him their only guide to take them beyond the ocean of ignorance and misery. There he sat in the glory of his own all-illumining realisation diffusing the balmy rays of his inner light by means of his most sweet and musical voice, all about him, softly raising and opening the lotus buds of the hearts of his ardent devotees. Peace reigned all around him. Blessed indeed were those few fortunate souls who had the rare privilege of sitting at the feet of such a great sage and Guru.

The cyclonic monk was not there carrying everything before him. There sat the peaceful

Preface

Rishi mildly disseminating the messages of peace and bliss to a few ardent souls fully ripe to receive them. How illumining and solacing were those sweet words coming out of his holy mouth like the smiling and breezy Dawn coming out of the lap of the bright and ruddy east and driving away the darkness before her. If those words had the power to console a few souls, they must have the power to bring comfort to all souls and blessed be the mother-heart of that loving disciple who preserved those saving words and did not allow them to be lost in the abysmal womb of Eternity. To mother Haridâsi (Miss S. Ellen Waldo) the whole world should be grateful for these "inspired" talks of Swamiji which have brought into existence the present volume. There cannot be a better friend and a better guide to all humanity than this. Whoever will taste the nectar in it is sure to know that death has no power over him.

Preface

May every soul seeking for illumination, rest and peace have recourse to it to end his or her miseries once for all.

MADRAS, 9th December 1910. — RAMAKRISHNÂNANDA.

PREFACE TO THE FIRST EDITION

All who had the blessing of personal contact with Swâmi Vivekânanda are of one accord that those who knew him on the lecture platform only, had but a small measure of his true power and greatness. It was in familiar conversation with chosen friends and disciples that came his most brilliant flashes of illumination, his loftiest flights of eloquence, his utterances of profoundest wisdom. Unfortunâtely, however, his printed works so far have shown us only Vivekânanda the lecturer ; Vivekânanda the friend, the teacher. the loving master, was known only to the happy few who had the rare privilege of sitting at his feet. Glimpses of this side of the great spiritual genius are revealed to us, it is true, in his published letters ; but the present volume is the first to give us words spoken by him in the intimacy of an inner circle.

They were taken down by Miss S. E. Waldo of New York, who from the early days of the Swâmi's American mission served him with unremitting devotion. It was to her that he dictated his translation and explanation of Pantanjali's Aphorisms, published in his "Râja Yoga," and often has she told me how she would sit for long periods of time watching always to see that the ink on her pen was kept wet, ready to write down the first word that would come as the Swâmi would emerge from the depths of self-contemplation into which he had plunged, to discover the true meaning of the terse Sanskrit phrases. It was she also who prepared all his American publications for the press ; and so great was Swâmi Vivekânanda's confidence in her ability, that he would pass the type written transcriptions of his lectures over to her with the instruction to do with them what she thought best, for his own indifference to the fruits of his work was so extreme, that he could not be induced to give even a cursory glance at his recorded words.

Through this constant faithful service with heart and brain, the disciple's mind became so at one with the master's that, even without the aid of shorthand, she was able to transcribe his teaching with wonderful fullness and accuracy. As she herself said, it was as if the thought of Swâmi Vivekânanda flowed through her and wrote itself upon the page. Once when she was reading a portion of these same notes to some tardy arrivals in the Thousand Island Park home, the Swâmi paced up down the floor, apparently unconscious of what was going on, until the travellers had left the room; then he turned to her and said: "How could you have caught my thought and words so perfectly? It was as if I heard myself speaking." What need of other commendation?

The Râmakrishna Mission of Madras is highly gratified in having been entrusted with the task of presenting these truly Inspired Talks to the public, and it wishes to express its heart-felt gratitude to each one of those who have aided in making this rich treasure, so long hidden, the property of all mankind.

MADRAS, DEVAMATA.
November 1908.

I

INTRODUCTORY NARRATIVE

In the summer of 1893 there landed in Vancouver a young Hindu *Sanyâsin*.* He was on his way to attend the Parliament of Religions at Chicago, but not as an accredited delegate from any recognised religious organisation. Unknown and inexperienced, he had been chosen for his mission by a few earnest young men of Madras, who firm in their belief that he, better than any one, could worthily represent the ancient religion of India, had

---

* Literally " one who has renounced "—the Hindu name for a man who gives up everything and devotes himself to the religious life either as a hermit or as a wandering religious teacher.

gone from door to door, soliciting money for his journey. The amount thus collected, together with contributions from one or two princes, enabled the youthful monk, the then obscure Swâmi Vivekânanda, to set out on his long journey.

It required tremendous courage to venture forth on such a mission. To leave the sacred soil of India for a foreign country means far more to a Hindu than we of the West can realize. Especially is this the case with a *Sanyâsin*, whose whole training is away from the practical, material side of life. Unused to handling money, or to any mode of travel save on his own feet, the Swâmi was robbed and imposed upon at every stage of his journey, until when he finally reached Chicago he was nearly penniless. He had brought with him no letters of introduction and knew no one in the great city.* Thus alone among strangers, thousands of miles from his own country, it was a situation to daunt even a strong man ; but the Swâmi left the matter in the hands of the Lord, firm in his faith that Divine protection would never fail him.

For nearly a fortnight he was able to meet the exorbitant demands of his hotel-keeper and others. Then the small sum still in his possession was reduced to such meagre proportions that he realized that, if he did not wish to die of starvation in the street, he must at once seek a place where the cost of living would be less.

* Later a Brahmin of Madras wrote to a gentleman in Chicago about the Swâmi and this gentleman took the young Hindu into his own family. Thus was begun a friendship which lasted as long as Swâmi Vivekânanda lived. All the members of the family learned to dearly love the Swâmi, to appreciate his brilliant gifts and to admire the purity and simplicity of his character, to which they often bore willing and loving testimony.

It was very hard for him to abandon the task which he had so bravely undertaken. For a moment a wave of discouragement and doubt swept over him and he began to wonder why he had been so foolish as to listen to those few hot-headed school-boys of Madras. Yet since no other course was left to him, with a sad heart he set out for Boston, determined to cable for money and, if need be, return to India.

But the Lord, in whom he so firmly trusted, willed otherwise. On the train he met an old lady and so far awakened her friendly interest that she invited him to become a guest in her house. Here he made the acquaintance of a professor from Harvard University, who after being closeted with the Swâmi for four hours one day, was so deeply impressed with his rare ability that he asked him why he did not represent Hinduism at the Chicago Parliament of Religions.

The Swâmi explained his difficulties,—that he had neither money nor letter of introduction to any one connected with the Parliament. "Mr. Bonney is my friend ; I will give you a letter to him," the Professor quickly replied ; and at once he wrote it, declaring in the course of it that he had found this unknown Hindu monk "more learned than all our learned men put together." With this letter and a ticket presented by the Professor, the Swâmi returned to Chicago and was readily accepted as a delegate.

At last the day of the opening of the Parliament arrived and Swâmi Vivekânanda took his place in the line of Oriental delegates who filed out on the platform at the opening Session. His purpose was accomplished ; but as he caught sight of that vast audience, a sudden nervousness seized him. All the others had prepared speeches. He had none. What should he say to that great gathering of six or seven thousand men and women? Throughout the morning he kept putting off his turn to be introduced, whispering each time to the President, "Let some one else speak first." So again in the afternoon, until about five when Dr. Barrows rising, named him as the next speaker.

The shock steadied the nerves and stimulated the courage of Vivekânanda, and he at once rose to the occasion. It was the first time in his life that he had ever stood upon his feet to speak, or had addressed a large audience, but the effect was electric. When he looked over the sea of expectant faces, he was filled with power and eloquence, and beginning in his musical voice, he addressed his hearers as "Sisters and Brothers of America." His success was immediate and during all the rest of the Congress his popularity never waned. He was always eagerly listened to and people would remain to the end of a long Session on a hot day in order to hear him.

This was the beginning of his work in the United States. After the Parliament was over, in order to provide for his necessities, the Swâmi accepted an offer from a Lecture Bureau to make a tour through the West. Although he attracted large audiences, he soon gave up the uncongenial work. He was here as a religious teacher, not as a popular lecturer on secular subjects; so he quickly abandoned a most profitable career and early in 1894 came to New York to start on his real mission. He first visited friends whom he had made in Chicago. They were chiefly among the wealthier class and he spoke now and then in their parlors; but this too failed to satisfy him. He felt that the interest he awakened was not what he wanted; it was too superficial, too much mere amusement-seeking. Therefore he decided to have a place of his own, where all earnest truth-seekers, whether rich or poor, would be free to come.

A lecture before the Brooklyn Ethical Association led naturally to this independent teaching. Dr. Lewis G. Janes, the President of the Association, had heard the young Hindu monk and, much attracted by his ability as well as by his message to us of the Western Hemisphere, had invited him to speak before the Association. It was on the last day of 1894. A large audience filled the Pouch Mansion, where the Ethical Association then held its meetings. The lecture was on "Hinduism" and as the Swâmi, in his long robe and turban, expounded the ancient religion of his native land, the interest grew so deep that at the close of the evening there was an insistent demand for regular classes in Brooklyn. The Swâmi graciously acceded and a series of class meetings was held and several public lectures were given in the Pouch Mansion and elsewhere.

A few of those who had heard him in Brooklyn now began to go to the place where he lived in New York. It was just an ordinary room on the second floor of a lodging house, and as the classes rapidly increased beyond the capacity of the chairs and one lounge, students sat on the dresser, on the corner marble washbasin and still others on the floor, like the Swâmi himself, who thus seated cross-legged after the manner of his own country, taught his eager students the great truths of Vedânta.

At last he felt that he was fairly started on his mission, which was to deliver to the Western world the message of his Master, Sri Râmakrishna, which proclaimed the truth and fundamental unity of all religions. The classes grew so rapidly that they soon overflowed the small upstairs room, and the large double parlors below were engaged. In them the Swâmi taught until the end of the season. The teaching was entirely free, the necessary expenses being met by voluntary contributions. These proving insufficient to pay the rent and provide for the maintenance of the Swâmi, the classes came near ending for want of pecuniary support. At once the Swâmi announced a course of public lectures on secular subjects for which he could receive remuneration, and so earned the money to support the religious classes. He explained that the Hindus regarded it as the duty of a religious teacher not only to freely give his teaching, but also if he possibly could, to bear the expenses of his work. In former times in India, it was even customary for the teacher to provide a home and food for his students.

By this time some of the students had become so deeply interested in the Swâmi's teachings that they were desirous to have them continued through the summer. He, however was tired after a hard season's work and at first demurred against prolonging his labors through the hot weather. Then too, many of the students would be out of town at this time of year. The problem solved itself. One of our number owned a small cottage at Thousand Island Park, the largest island in the St. Lawrence River; and she offered the use of it to the Swâmi and as many of us as it would accommodate. This plan appealed to the Swâmi and he agreed to join us there after a brief visit to the Maine Camp of one of his friends.

Miss D., the student to whom the cottage belonged, feeling that a special sanctuary should be prepared for the occasion, built as a true love offering to her Teacher, a new wing that was nearly as large as the original cottage.

The place was ideally situated on high ground, overlooking a wide sweep of the beautiful river with many of its far-famed Thousand Islands. Clayton could be dimly discerned in the distance, while the nearer and wider Canadian shores bounded the view to the north. The cottage stood on the side of a hill, which on the north and west sloped abruptly down towards the shores of the river and of a little inlet that like a small lake lay behind the house. The house itself was literally "built upon a rock," and huge bowlders lay all around it. The new wing stood on the steep slope of the rocks like a great lantern tower with windows on three sides, three stories deep at the back, and only two in the front. The lower room was occupied by one of the students. The one over it opened out of the main part of the house by several doors, and being large and convenient, became our class-room, where for hours each day the Swâmi gave us familiar instruction. Over this room was the one devoted exclusively to the use of the Swâmi. In order that it might be perfectly secluded, Miss D. had supplied it with a separate outside staircase, although there was also a door opening upon the second story of the piazza.

This upstairs piazza played an important part in our lives, as all the Swâmi's evening talks were given here. It was wide and roomy, roofed in, and extended along the south and west sides of the cottage. Miss D. had the west side of it carefully screened off by a partition, so that none of the strangers who frequently visited the piazza to see the magnificent view it commanded, could intrude upon our privacy. There, close by his own door, sat our beloved Teacher every evening during our stay and communed with us who sat silent in the darkness, eagerly drinking in his inspired words. The place was a veritable sanctuary. At our feet, like a sea of green, waved the leaves of the tree tops, for the entire place was surrounded by thick woods. Not one house of the large village could be seen, it was as if we were in the heart of some dense forest, miles away from the haunts of men. Beyond the trees spread the wide expanse of the St. Lawrence, dotted here and there with islands, some of which gleamed bright with the lights of hotels and boarding-houses. All these were so far away that they seemed more like a pictured scene than a reality. Not a human sound penetrated our seclusion; we heard but the murmur of the insects, the sweet songs of the birds, or the gentle sighing of the wind through the leaves. Part of the time the scene was illumined by the soft rays of the moon and her face was mirrored in the shining waters beneath. In this scene of enchantment, "the world forgetting, by the world forgot," we spent seven blessed weeks with our beloved Teacher, listening to his words of inspiration. Immediately after our evening meal each day of our stay, we all repaired to the upper piazza and awaited the coming of our Master. Nor had we long to wait, for hardly had we assembled ere the door of his room would open and he would quietly step out and take his accustomed seat. He always spent two hours with us and more often much longer. One glorious night, when the moon was about the full, he talked to us until she set below the western horizon, apparently as unconscious as we were of the lapse of time.

Of these talks it was not possible to take notes. They are preserved only in the hearts of the hearers. None of us can ever forget the uplift, the intense spiritual life of those hallowed hours. The Swâmi poured out all his heart at those times, his own struggles were enacted again before us; the very spirit of his Master seemed to speak through his lips, to satisfy all doubts, to answer all questioning, to soothe every fear. Many times the Swâmi seemed hardly conscious of our presence, and then we almost held our breath for fear of disturbing him and checking the flow of his thoughts. He would rise from his seat and pace up and down the narrow limits of the piazza, pouring forth a perfect torrent of eloquence. Never was he more gentle, more loveable than during these hours. It may have been much like the way his own great Master taught his disciples, just allowing them to listen to the outpourings of his own spirit in communion with himself.

It was a perpetual inspiration to live with a man like Swâmi Vivekânanda. From morning till night it was ever the same, we lived in a constant atmosphere of intense spirituality

Often playful and fun-loving, full of merry jest and quick repartee, he was never for a moment far from the dominating note of his life. Everything could furnish a text or an illustration, and in a moment we would find ourselves swept from amusing tales of Hindu mythology to the deepest philosophy. The Swâmi had an inexhaustible fund of mythological lore and surely no race is more abundantly supplied with myths than those ancient Aryans. He loved to tell them to us and we delighted to listen, for he never failed to point out the reality hidden under myth and story and to draw from it valuable spiritual lessons. Never had fortunate students greater cause to congratulate themselves on having so gifted a Teacher!

By a singular coincidence just twelve students followed the Swâmi to Thousand Island Park, and he told us that he accepted us as real disciples and that was why he so constantly and freely taught us, giving us his best. All the twelve were not together at once, ten being the largest number present at any one time. Two of our number subsequently became *sanyâsins,* both being initiated at Thousand Island Park. On the occasion of the consecration of the second *sanyâsin,* Swâmi initiated five of us as *brahmacharins,** and later, in New York City, the rest of our number took initiation, together with several other of the Swâmi's disciples there.

It was decided, when we went to Thousand Island Park, that we should live as a community, each doing his or her share of the house-work in order that no alien presence should mar the serenity of our household. The Swâmi himself was an accomplished cook and often prepared for us delicious dishes. He had learned how to cook when, after his Master's death, he had

* Religious students devoted to a particular teacher.

served his brethren, a band of young men, his fellow-disciples, whom he held together and taught, continuing the training begun by his Master, in order that they might be fitted to spread abroad over the world the truths imparted by Sri Râmakrishna.

Every morning, just as soon as our various tasks were over (and often before), the Swâmi called us together in the large parlor that served us as class-room and began to teach us. Each day he took up some special subject, or expounded from some sacred book, as the *Bhagavad Gitâ*, the *Upanishads*, or the *Vedânta Sutras* of Vyâsa. The *Sutras* are in the form of aphorisms, being the briefest possible statements of the great truths imbedded in the Vedas. They have neither nominative nor verb, and so intent were the writers of them on eliminating every unnecessary word, that a Hindu proverb says that "a writer of *Sutras* would rather give one of his sons than add a syllable to his *sutra.*"

Because of their almost enigmatical brevity the *Vedânta Sutras* offer a rich field for the commentator, and three great Hindu philosophers, Sankara, Râmânuja, and Madhva, wrote elaborate commentaries upon them. In his morning talks the Swâmi would take up first one of these commentaries, then another, showing how each commentator was guilty of twisting the meaning of the *Sutras* to meet his own particular view, and would read in the aphorism whatever would best substantiate his own interpretation. The Swâmi often pointed out to us how old is the bad habit of "text-torturing."

Thus it was that in these lessons the point of view presented was some times that of pure dualism as represented by Madhva, while on another day it was that of the qualified non-dualism taught by Râmânuja, known as *Visishtâdvaita.* Most frequently, however, the monistic commentary of Sankara was taken up ; but because of his subtlety he was more difficult to understand, so to the end Râmânuja remained the favourite among the students.

Sometimes the Swâmi took up the *Bhakti Sutras* of Nârada. They are a short exposition of devotion to God, which gives one some conception of the lofty Hindu ideal of real, all-absorbing love for the Lord, love that literally possesses the devotee to the exclusion of every other thought. *Bhakti* is the Hindu method of realizing union with the Divine, a method which naturally appeals to the devout. It is to love God and Him only.

In these talks the Swâmi for the first time spoke to us at length about his great Master, Sri Râmakrishna, of his daily life with him and of his struggles with his own tendency to unbelief, which at times drew tears from his Master. The other disciples have often said that Sri Râmakrishna always told them that Swâmi Vivekânanda was a great Soul, who had come especially to help his work and that as soon as he knew who he really was, he would, at once give up the body. But he added that before that time arrived, there was a certain mission which the Swâmi would have to accomplish, to help not only India but other lands as well. Frequently Sri Râmakrishna said, "I have other disciples far away, who speak a language I do not understand."

After seven weeks spent at Thousand Island Park, the Swâmi returned to New York City and later went abroad. He lectured and held classes in England until the end of November, when he returned to New York and resumed his teaching there. On this occasion, his students secured a competent stenographer and thus preserved the Swami's words. The reports of the class lectures were soon after published in book form and these books, together with the pamphlets of the public lectures, remain to-day as enduring monuments of Swâmi Vivekânanda's work in America. To those of us who were privileged to hear the lectures given, the Swâmi's very presence seems to live again and to speak to us from the printed pages, so exactly and accurately were his utterances transcribed by one, who subsequently became one of the Swâmi's most devoted disciples. The work of both Teacher and taught was purely a labor of love, so the blessing of the Lord rested upon it.

S. E. W.

NEW YORK, 1908.

II

THE MASTER.

February 14th, 1894, stands out in my memory as a day apart, a sacred, holy day ; for it was then that I first saw the form and listened to the voice of that Great Soul, that Spiritual Giant, the Swami Vivekânanda who, two years later, to my great joy and never-ceasing wonder, accepted me as a disciple.

He had been lecturing in the large cities of this country and on the above date gave the first of a series of lectures in Detroit, in the Unitarian Church. The large edifice was literally packed and the Swâmi received an ovation. I can see him yet as he stepped upon the platform, a regal, majestic figure, vital, forceful, dominant, and at the first sound of the wonderful voice, a voice all music—now like the plaintive minor strain of an Eolian harp, again, deep, vibrant, resonant—there was a hush, a stillness that could almost be felt, and the vast audience breathed as one man.

The Swâmi gave five public lectures and he held his audiences, for his was the grasp of the "master hand" and he spoke as one with authority. His arguments were logical, convincing, and in his most brilliant oratorical flights never once did he lose sight of the main issue,—the truth he wished to drive home.

He fearlessly attacked principles, but in personal matters one felt that here was a man whose great heart could take in all of humanity, seeing beyond their faults and foibles; one who would suffer and forgive to the uttermost. In fact, when it was given to me to know him more intimately, I found that he *did* forgive to the uttermost. With what infinite love and patience would he lead those who came to him, out of the labyrinth of their own frailties and point out to them the way out of self to God. He knew no malice. Did one abuse him, he would look thoughtful, repeat *Siva, Siva,* then his face would become illumined and he would say gently: " It is only the voice of the Beloved;" or if we who loved him would become indignant, he would ask: "What difference can it make when one knows that blamer, blamed, and praiser, praised, are one ? " Again, under like circumstances he would tell us some story of how Sri Râmakrishna would never recognise personal abuse or malice. Everything good or bad, " the dual throng," was from the " Beloved Mother. "

It was given to me to know him in an intimate way for a period of several years and never once did I find a flaw in his character.

He was incapable of petty weakness and had Vivekânanda possessed faults, they would have been generous ones. With all his greatness he was as simple as a child, equally at home among the rich and the great, or among the poor and the lowly.

While in Detroit he was the guest of Mrs. John J. Bagley, the widow of the ex-Governor of Michigan and a lady of rare culture and unusual spirituality. She told me that never once during the time he was a guest in her house (about four weeks) did he fail to express the highest in word and action, that his presence was a "continual benediction." After leaving Mrs. Bagley, Vivekânanda spent two weeks as the guest of Hon. Thomas W. Palmer. Mr. Palmer was President of the World's Fair Commission; he had been formerly U. S. Minister to Spain and also a U. S. Senator. This gentleman is still living and is over eighty years of age.

For myself, I can say that never in all the years I knew Vivekânanda did he fail to manifest the highest in life and purpose.

Blessed and beloved Swâmiji, I never thought it possible for man to be so white, so chaste, as he was! It set him apart from other men. He was brought in contact with our most brilliant and beautiful women, mere beauty did not attract him but he would often say: "I like to cross swords with your bright intellectual women; it is a new experience for me, for in my country the women are more or less secluded."

His manner was that of boyish frankness and *naivete'* and very winsome. I remember one evening after he had delivered a profoundly impressive lesson, scaling the very heights of realization, he was found standing at the foot of the stairs with a puzzled, almost disconsolate expression on his face. People were going up and down stairs putting on their wraps, etc. Suddenly his face lighted up and he said: "I have it! going up the stairs, the gentleman precedes the lady,—coming down, the lady precedes the gentleman, isn't it?" True to his Eastern training, he felt that a breach of etiquette was a breach of hospitality.

In speaking to me one day regarding those who wished to have a part in his life work, he said "they must be pure in heart." There was one disciple of whom he hoped much. He evidently saw in her great possibilities for renunciation and self-sacrifice. He found me alone one day and asked me many questions regarding her life and environment, and after I had answered them all, he looked at me so wistfully and said: "And she is pure, pure in soul, is it not?" I simply answered: "Yes Swâmi, she is absolutely pure in heart." His face lighted up and his eyes shone with divine fire ;—" I knew it, I felt it, I must have her for my work in Calcutta," he said with enthusiasm.

He then told me of his plans and hopes for the advancement of the women of India. " Education is what they need," he would say, " We must have a school in Calcutta." A school for girls has since been established there by the Sister Nivedita and the above-mentioned disciple shares the work with her, living in a Calcutta lane and wearing the *Sari*, doing the Mother's work as best she may. She shared all these experiences with me, for we together sought out the Master and asked him to teach us. He was the " man of the hour " in Detroit that winter. Society smiled upon him and he was much sought after. The daily papers recorded his comings and his goings ; even his food was discussed, one paper gravely stating that his breakfast consisted of bread and butter thickly sprinkled with pepper ! Letters and invitations came pouring in and Detroit was at the feet of Vivekânanda.

He always loved Detroit and was grateful for all the kindness and courtesy shown him. We had no chance to meet him in a personal way at the time, but we listened and pondered in our hearts over all that we heard him say, resolving to find him sometime, somewhere, even if we had to go across the world to do it. We lost trace of him completely for nearly two years and thought that probably he had returned to India, but one afternoon we were told by a friend that he was still in this country and that he was spending the summer at Thousand Island Park. We started the next morning, resolved to seek him out and ask him to teach us.

At last after a weary search, we found him. We were feeling very much frightened at our temerity in thus intruding upon his privacy, but he had lighted a fire in our souls that could not be quenched. We must know more of this wonderful man and his teaching. It was a dark and rainy night and we were weary after our long journey, but we could not rest until we had seen him face to face. Would he accept us ? And if he did not, what then could we do ? It suddenly seemed to us that it might be a foolish thing to go several hundred miles to find a man who did not even know of our existence, but we plodded on up the hill in the rain and darkness, with a man we had hired to show us the way with his lantern. Speaking of this in after years, our Guru would refer to us as "my disciples, who travelled hundreds of miles to find me and they came in the night and in the rain." We had thought of what to say to him, but when we realized that we had really found him, we instantly forgot all our fine speeches and one of us blurted out : "We came from Detroit and Mrs. P. sent us to you." The other said : "We have come to you just as we would go to Jesus if he were still on the earth and ask him to teach us.'' He looked at us so kindly and said gently, "If only I possessed the power of the Christ to set you free now !" He stood for a moment looking thoughtful and then turning to his hostess who was standing near, said : "These ladies are from Detroit, please show them upstairs and allow them to spend the evening with us." We remained until late listening to the Master who paid no more attention to us, but as we bade them all good night we were told to come the next morning at nine o'clock. We arrived promptly, and to our great joy were accepted by the Master and were cordially invited to become members of the household.

Of our stay there another disciple has written fully, and I will only say that it was a most blessed summer. I have never seen our Master quite as he was then. He was at his best among those who loved him.

There were twelve of us and it seemed as if Pentecostal fire descended and touched the Master. One afternoon when he had been telling us of the glory of renunciation, of the joy and freedom of those of the ochre robe, he suddenly left us and in a short time he had written his "Song of the *Sanyâsin,*" a very passion of sacrifice and renunciation. I think the thing which impressed me most in those days was his infinite patience and gentleness—like a father with his children, though most of us were several years older than he. After a morning in the class-room where it almost seemed as if he had gazed into the very face of the Infinite, he would leave the room returning soon to say: "Now I am going to cook for you." And with what patience would he stand over the stove and prepare some Indian tit-bit for us! The last time he was with us in Detroit he prepared for us the most delicious curries. What a lesson to his disciples,—the brilliant, the great and learned Vivekânanda ministering to their little wants! He was at those times so gentle, so benign. What a legacy of sacred tender memories has he left us!

One day Vivekânanda related to us the story that had most impressed itself upon his life. It was told him over and over again in his babyhood by his nurse and he never wearied of hearing it repeated. I will give it as nearly as possible in his own words.

The widow of a Brahmin was left very, very poor with one child, a little boy who was almost a baby. Because he was the son of a Brahmin the boy had to be educated, but how to do it? In the village where the poor widow lived, there was no teacher, so the boy had to go to the neighbouring village to be taught and because his mother was very, very poor he had to walk there. There was a small forest between the two villages and through this the boy had to pass. In India, as in all hot countries, teaching is given very early in the morning and again towards evening. Through the heat of the day no work is done, so it was always dark when the little boy went to school and also when be came home. In my country, instruction in religion is free to those who cannot pay, so the little boy could go to this teacher without charge, but he had to walk through the forest and he was all alone and he was terribly afraid. He went to his mother and said: "I have always to go alone through that terrible forest and I am afraid. Other boys have servants to go with them and take care of them, why cannot I have a servant to go with me?" But his mother said: "Alas my child ! I am too poor, I cannot send a servant with you." "What can I do then ?" asked the little boy. "I will tell you," said his mother, "do this. In the forest is your shepherd-brother Krishna (Krishna is known in India as the "shepherd-god") ; call on him and he will come and take care of you and you will not be alone." So the next day the little boy went into the forest and called "Brother-shepherd, brother-shepherd, are you there ?" and he heard a voice say "Yes, I am here," and the little boy was comforted and was no more afraid. By and by he used to meet, coming out of the forest, a boy of his own age who played with him and walked with him and the little boy was happy. After a while the father of the teacher died and their was a great ceremonial festival (as is common in India on such occasions), when all the scholars made presents to their teacher and the poor little boy went to his mother and asked her to buy him a present to give like the rest. But his mother told him she was too poor. Then he wept and said: "What shall I do?" And his mother said, "Go to brother-shepherd and ask him." So he went into the forest and called, "Brother-shepherd, brother-shepherd, can you give me a present to give to my teacher?" And there appeared before him a little pitcher of milk. The boy took the pitcher gratefully and went to the house of his teacher and stood in a corner waiting for the servants to take his gift to the teacher. But the other presents were so much grander and finer that the servants paid no attention to him, so he spoke and said, "Teacher, here is the present I have brought you." Still no one took any notice. Then the little boy spoke up again from his corner and said, "Teacher, here is the present I have brought you," and the teacher looking over and seeing the pitiful little gift, scorned it, but said to the servant, "Since he makes so much fuss about it, take the pitcher and pour the milk into one of the glasses and let him go." So the servant took the pitcher and poured the milk into a cup, but just as soon as he poured out the milk, the pitcher filled right up again and it could not be emptied. Then everybody was surprised and asked, " What is this, where did you get this pitcher ?" and the little boy said, " Brother-shepherd gave it to me in the forest." " What !" they all exclaimed, " you have seen Krishna and he gave you this ?" " Yes", said the little boy, " and he plays with me every day and walks with me when I come to school. " " What !" they all exclaimed " You walk with Krishna ! You play with Krishna !" And the teacher said, " Can you take us and show us this ?" And the little boy said, " Yes I can, come with me. " Then the little boy and the teacher went into the forest and the little boy began to call as usual,

"Brother-shepherd, brother-shepherd, here is my teacher come to you, where are you ?'' but no answer came. The little boy called again and again and no answer came. Then he wept and said, " Brother-shepherd do come, or else they will call me a liar." Then from afar off a voice was heard saying : " I come to you because you are pure and your time has come, but your teacher has many many rounds to go through before he can see Me."

After the summer at Thousand Island Park, Vivekânanda sailed for England and I did not see him until the following spring (1896) when he came to Detroit for two weeks. He was accompanied by his stenographer, the faithful Goodwin. They occupied a suite of rooms at *The Richelieu*, a small family hotel, and had the use of the large drawing room for class work and lectures. The room was not large enough to accommodate the crowds and to our great regret many were turned away. The room, as also the hall, staircase and library were literally packed. At that time he was all *Bhakti*—the love for God was a hunger and a thirst. A kind of divine madness seemed to take possession of him, as if his heart would burst with longing for the Beloved Mother.

His last public appearance in Detroit was at the Temple Beth El of which the Rabbi Louis Grossman, an ardent admirer of the Swâmi, was the pastor. It was Sunday evening and so great was the crowd that we almost feared a panic. There was a solid line reaching far out into the street and hundreds were turned away. Vivekânanda held the large audience spellbound, his subject being, "India's message to the West," and "The Ideal of a Universal Religion." He gave us a most brilliant and masterly discourse. Never had I seen the

Master look as he looked that night. There was something in his beauty not of earth. It was as if the spirit had almost burst the bonds of flesh and it was then that I first saw a foreshadowing of the end. He was much exhausted from years of overwork, and it was even then to be seen that he was not long for this world. I tried to close my eyes to it, but in my heart I knew the truth. He had needed rest but felt that he must go on.

The next time I saw him was in July 1899. He had been extremely ill and it was thought that a long sea voyage would benefit him, so he sailed for England from Calcutta on the steamship *Golconda*; much to his surprise, two of his American disciples were at the Tilbury Docks in London when the ship arrived. We had seen in an Indian magazine a notice that he would sail on a certain date and we hastened over to the other side to meet him, as we were very much alarmed at the reports we had heard regarding his health.

He had grown very slim and looked and acted like a boy. He was so happy to find the voyage had brought back some of the old strength and vigor. The Sister Nivedita and the Swâmi Turiyânanda accompanied him to England and quarters were found for the two Swâmis in a roomy old fashioned house at Wimbledon not far from London. It was very quiet and restful and we all spent a happy month there.

Swâmi did no public work in England at that time and soon sailed for America accompanied by the Swâmi Turiyânanda and his American friends. There were ten never-to-be-forgotten days spent on the ocean. Reading and exposition of the *Gitâ* occupied every morning, also reciting and translating poems and stories from the Sanskrit and chanting old

Vedic hymns. The sea was smooth and at night the moonlight was entrancing. Those were wonderful evenings; the Master paced up and down the deck, a majestic figure in the moonlight, stopping now and then to speak to us of the beauties of Nature. "And if all this *Mâyâ* is so beautiful, think of the wondrous beauty of the Reality behind it!" he would exclaim.

One especially fine evening when the moon was at the full and softly mellow and golden, a night of mystery and enchantment, he stood silently for a long time drinking in the beauty of the scene. Suddenly he turned to us and said: "Why recite poetry when there," pointing to sea and sky, "is the very essence of poetry?"

We reached New York all too soon, feeling that we never could be grateful enough for those blessed, intimate ten days with our Guru.

The next time I saw him was on July 4th, 1900, when he came to Detroit for a short visit among his friends.

He had grown so thin, almost ethereal,—not long would that great spirit be imprisoned in clay. Once more we closed our eyes to the sad truth, hoping against hope.

I never saw him again, but "that other disciple" was privileged to be with him in India for a few weeks before he left us for ever. Of that time I cannot bear to think. The sorrow and the heartbreak of it all still abides with me; but deep down underneath all the pain and grief is a great calm, a sweet and blessed consciousness that Great Souls do come to earth to point out to men "the way, the truth, and the life"; and when I realize that it was given to me to come under the influence of such an One, finding each day a new beauty, a deeper significance in his teachings, I can almost believe, as I meditate upon all this, that I hear a voice saying :—"Take off thy shoes from off thy feet for the place whereon thou standest is holy ground."

M. C. F.

DETROIT, MICHIGAN, 1908.

NOTE

At the morning talks it was possible to take a few notes and those that follow were made on these occasions. They are naturally somewhat disconnected as the Swâmi encouraged us to ask questions and to seek the fullest explanation of any problem that presented itself. Thus, these are not at all like notes of regular lectures, but simply brief records of familiar discourses. Being taken in longhand (and solely for individual use), much that was said failed to be written down. Such as they are, with all their incompleteness, they possess a value of their own, and an added value to those who knew and loved the Swâmi, as being his utterances. While necessarily the teaching itself cannot vary much, the presentation is new and different from anything that we now have in print of the words of our much loved Teacher.

In loving remembrance of a great and good man and of the many happy hours spent with him, these fragments of his teachings are now offered to the public. May the Lord whom he so devoutly worshipped and untiringly proclaimed to us, bless his inspired words and fill our hearts with that divine love which the Swâmi so constantly urged us to manifest !

S. E. W.

INSPIRED TALKS

INSPIRED TALKS

WEDNESDAY, *June 19th*, 1895.

(This day marks the beginning of the regular teaching given daily by Swâmi Vivekânanda to his disciples at Thousand Island Park. We had not yet all assembled there, but the Master's heart was always in his work, so he commenced at once to teach the three or four who were with him. He came on this first morning with the Bible in his hand and opened to the Book of John, saying that since we were all Christians, it was proper that he should begin with the Christian Scriptures.)

"In the beginning was the Word, and the Word was with God, and the Word was God." The Hindu calls this *Mâyâ*, the manifestation of God, because it is the power of God.* The Absolute reflecting through the universe is what we call Nature. The word has two manifestations,—the general one of Nature, and the special one of the great Incarnations of God—Krishna, Buddha, Jesus and Râmakrishna. Christ, the special manifestation of the Absolute, is known and knowable. The Absolute cannot be known: we cannot know the Father, only the Son. We can only see the Absolute through the "tint of humanity," through Christ.

In the first five verses of John is the whole essence of Christianity; each verse is full of the profoundest philosophy.

The Perfect never becomes imperfect. It is in the darkness, but is not affected by the darkness. God's mercy goes to all, but is not affected by their wickedness. The sun is not affected by any disease of our eyes which may make us see it distorted. In the

* *Ma'ya'* being the *Sakti* (power) of God.

twenty-ninth verse "taketh away the sin of the world" means that Christ would show us the way to become perfect. God became Christ to show man his true nature, that we too are God. We are human coverings over the Divine, but as the divine Man, Christ and we are one.

The Trinitarian Christ is elevated above us; the Unitarian Christ is merely a moral man; neither can help us. The Christ who is the Incarnation of God, who has not forgotten His divinity, that Christ can help us, in Him there is no imperfection. These Incarnations are always conscious of their own divinity; they know it from their birth. They are like the actors whose play is over, but who, after their work is done, return to please others. These great Ones are untouched by aught of earth; they assume our form and our limitations for a time in order to teach us, but in reality they are never limited, they are ever free.

* * * *

Good is near Truth, but is not yet Truth. After learning not to be disturbed by evil, we have to learn not to be made happy by good. We must find that we are beyond both evil and good; we must study their adjustment and see that they are both necessary.

The idea of dualism is from the ancient Persians.* Really good and evil are one,† and are in our own mind. When the mind is self-poised neither good nor bad affects it. Be perfectly free, then neither can affect it, and we enjoy freedom and bliss. Evil is the iron chain, good is the gold one; both are chains. Be free, and know once for all that there is no chain for

---

* Parsees, the followers of Zoroaster who taught that the whole creation has come out of two primary principles, one being called *Ormuzd* (the principle of Good) and the other *Ahriman* (the principle of Evil.)

† Because they are both chains.

you. Lay hold of the golden chain to loosen the hold of the iron one, then throw both away. The thorn of evil is in our flesh; take another thorn from the same bush and extract the first thorn, then throw away both and be free.

*　*　*　*　*

In the world take always the position of the giver. Give everything and look for no return. Give love, give help, give service, give any little thing you can, but *keep out barter.* Make no conditions and none will be imposed. Let us give out of our own bounty, just as God gives to us.

The Lord is the only Giver, all the world are only shopkeepers. Get His cheque and it must be honored everywhere.

"God is the inexplicable, inexpressible essence of Love," to be known, but never defined.

*　*　*　*　*

In our miseries and struggles the world seems to us a very dreadful place. But just as when we watch two puppies playing and biting we do not concern ourselves at all, realizing that it is only fun and that even a sharp nip now and then will do no actual harm ; so all our struggles are but play in God's eyes. This world is all for play and only amuses God ; nothing in it can make God angry.

* * * *

"Mother ! In the sea of life my bark is sinking,
The whirlwind of illusion, the storm of attachment is growing every moment,
My five oarsmen (senses) are foolish, and the helmsman (mind) is weak.
My bearings are lost, my boat is sinking.
O Mother ! Save me !"

"Mother, Thy light stops not for the saint or the sinner; it animates the lover and the murderer.'' Mother is ever manifesting through all. The light is not polluted by what it shines on, nor benefited by it. The light is ever pure, ever changeless. Behind every creature is the "Mother," pure, lovely, never changing. "Mother! manifested as light in all beings, we bow down to Thee!" She is equally in suffering, hunger, pleasure, sublimity. "When the bee sucks honey, the Lord is eating." Knowing that the Lord is everywhere, the sages give up praising and blaming. *Know* that nothing can hurt you. How? Are you not free? Are you not *A'tman*? He is the Life of our lives, the hearing of our ears, the sight of our eyes.

We go through the world like a man pursued by a policeman and see the barest glimpses of the beauty of it. All this fear that pursues us comes from believing in matter. Matter gets its whole existence from the presence of mind behind it. What we see is God percolating through nature.*

SUNDAY, *June 23rd*

Be brave and be sincere ; then follow any path with devotion and you *must* reach the Whole. Once lay hold of one link of the chain and the whole chain must come by degrees. Water the roots of the tree, (that is, reach the Lord) and the whole tree is watered ; getting the Lord, we get all.

One-sideness is the bane of the world. The more sides you can develop, the more souls you have and you can see the universe through all souls,—through the *Bhakta,* (devotee) and the *Jnâni* (philosopher). Determine your own nature and stick to it. *Nishthâ* (devotion to one ideal) is the only method for the beginner, but with devotion and sincerity it will lead to all. Churches, doctrines, forms are the hedges to

* Here "Nature' means matter and mind. (Ed.)

protect the tender plant, but they must later be broken down that the plant may become a tree. So the various religions, Bibles, Vedas, dogmas all are just tubs for the little plant; but it must get out of the tub. *Nishthâ* is, in a manner, placing the plant in the tub, shielding the struggling soul in its chosen path.

* * * *

Look at the "ocean" and not at the "wave"; see no difference between ant and angel. Every worm is the brother of the Nazarene. How say one is greater and one less? Each is great, in his own place. We are in the sun and in the stars as much as here. Spirit is beyond space and time, and is everywhere. Every mouth praising the Lord is my mouth, every eye seeing is my eye. We are confined nowhere; we are not body, the universe is our body. We are magicians waving magic wands and creating scenes before us at will. We are the spider in his huge web, who can go on the varied strands wheresoever he desires. The spider is now only conscious of the spot where he is, but he will in time become conscious of the whole web. We are now conscious only where the body is, we can use only one brain ; but when we reach ultra-consciousness, we know all, we can use all brains. Even now we can "give the push" in consciousness and it goes beyond and acts in the superconscious.

We are striving "to be" and nothing more, no "I" even,—just pure crystal, reflecting *all*, but ever the same. When that state is reached there is no more doing ; the body becomes a mere mechanism, pure without care for it ; it cannot become impure.

Know you are the Infinite, then fear must die. Say ever "I and my Father are one."

* * * *

In time to come Christs will be in numbers

like bunches of grapes on a vine ; then the play will be over and all will pass out. As water in a kettle beginning to boil shows first one bubble then another, then more and more until all is in ebullition and passes out as steam. Buddha and Christ are the two biggest "bubbles" the world has yet produced. Moses was a tiny bubble, greater and greater ones came. Sometime however all will be bubbles and escape ; but creation, ever new, will bring new water to go through the process all over again.

MONDAY, *June 24th.* (*The reading to-day was from the Bhakti Sutras by Nârada.*)

" Extreme love to God is Bhakti, and this love is the real immortality, getting which a man becomes perfectly satisfied, sorrows for no loss and is never jealous ; knowing which man becomes mad."

My Master used to say, " this world is a huge

lunatic asylum where all men are mad, some after money, some after women, some after name or fame, and a few after God. I prefer to be mad after God. God is the philosopher's stone that turns us to gold in an instant; the form remains, but the nature is changed—the human form remains, but no more can we hurt or sin."

"Thinking of God, some weep, some sing, some laugh, some dance, some say wonderful things, but all speak of nothing but God."

Prophets preach, but the Incarnations like Jesus, Buddha, Râmakrishna, can *give* religion; one glance, one touch is enough. That is the power of the Holy Ghost, the "laying on of hands"; the power was actually transmitted to the disciples by the Master,—the "chain of Guru-power." That, the real baptism, has been handed down for untold ages.

"Bhakti cannot be used to fulfil any desires, itself being the check to all desires." Nârada gives these as the signs of love. "When all thoughts, all words and all deeds are given up unto the Lord, and the least forgetfulness of God makes one intensely miserable, then love has begun."

"This is the highest form of love because therein is no desire for reciprocity, which desire is in all human love."

"A man who has gone beyond social and Scriptural usage, he is a *Sanyâsin*. When the whole soul goes to God, when we take refuge only in God, then we know that we are about to get this love."

Obey the Scriptures until you are strong enough to do without them, then go beyond them. Books are not an end-all. Verification is the only proof of religious truth. Each must verify for himself; and no teacher who says "I have seen, but *you* cannot" is to be trusted, only that one who says "you can see too." All

Scriptures, all truths are Vedas, in all times, in all countries ; because these truths are to be *seen* and any one may discover them.

"When the sun of Love begins to break on the horizon, we want to give up all our actions unto God and when we forget Him for a moment, it grieves us greatly."

Let nothing stand between God and your love for Him. Love Him, love Him, love Him, and let the world say what it will. Love is of three sorts,—one demands, but gives nothing ; the second is exchange, and the third is love without thought of return, love like that of the moths for the light.

"Love is higher than works, than *Yoga*, than knowledge."

Work is merely a schooling for the doer, it can do no good to others. We must work out our own problem, the prophets only show us how to work. "What you think, you become," so if you throw your burden on Jesus, you will have to think of Him and thus become like Him, you *love* Him.

"Extreme love and highest knowledge are one."

But theorizing about God will not do; we must love and work. Give up the world and all wordly things, especially while the "plant" is tender. Day and night think of God and think of nothing else as far as possible. The daily necessary thoughts can all be thought through God. Eat to Him, drink to Him, sleep to Him, see Him in all. Talk of God to others, this is most beneficial.

Get the mercy of God and of His greatest children; these are the two chief ways to God. The company of these children of light is very hard to get; five minutes in their company will change a whole life, and if you really want it enough, one will come to you. The presence of those who love God makes a place holy, "such is the glory of the children of the Lord." They are He; and when they speak, their words are Scriptures. The place where they have been becomes filled with their vibrations, and those going there feel them and have a tendency to become holy also.

"To such lovers there is no distinction of caste, learning, beauty, birth, wealth, or occupation; because all are His."

Give up all evil company, especially at the beginning. Avoid worldly company, that will distract your mind. Give up all "me and mine." To him who has nothing in the universe the Lord comes. Cut the bondage of all worldly affections; go beyond laziness and all care as to what becomes of you. Never turn back to see the result of what you have done. Give all to the Lord and go on and think not of it. The whole soul pours in a continuous current to God ; there is no time to seek money, or name, or fame, no time to think of anything but God ; then will come into our hearts that infinite, wonderful bliss of Love. All desires are but beads of glass. Love of God increases every moment and is ever new, to be known only by feeling it. Love is the easiest of all, it waits for no logic, it is natural. We need no demonstration, no proof. Reasoning is limiting something by our own minds. We throw a net and catch something, and then say that we have demonstrated it ; but never, never can we catch God in a net.

Love should be unrelated. Even when we love wrongly, it is of the true love, of the true bliss ; the power is the same, use it as we may. Its very nature is peace and bliss. The murderer when he kisses his baby forgets for an instant all but love. Give up all self, all egotism; get out of anger, lust, give *all* to God. "I am not, but Thou art; the old man is all gone, only Thou remainest." "I am Thou." Blame none; if evil comes, know the Lord is playing with you and be exceeding glad.

Love is beyond time and space, it is absolute.

TUESDAY, *June 25th.*

After every happiness comes misery; they may be far apart or near. The more advanced the soul, the more quickly does one follow the other. What we want is neither happiness nor misery. Both make us forget our true nature; both are chains, one iron, one gold; behind both is the Âtman, Who knows neither happiness nor misery. These are *states* and states must ever change; but the nature of the soul is bliss, peace unchanging. We have not to get it, we have it; only wash away the dross and see it.

Stand upon the Self, then only can we truly

love the world. Take a very, very high stand; knowing our universal nature, we must look with perfect calmness upon all the panorama of the world. It is but baby's play, and we know that, so cannot be disturbed by it. If the mind is pleased with praise, it will be displeased with blame. All pleasures of the senses or even of the mind are evanescent, but within ourselves is the one true unrelated pleasure, dependent upon nothing. It is perfectly free, it is bliss. The more our bliss is within, the more spiritual we are. The pleasure of the Self is what the world calls religion.

The internal universe, the *real,* is infinitely greater than the external, which is only a shadowy projection of the true one. This world is neither true nor untrue, it is the shadow of truth. "Imagination is the gilded shadow of truth," says the poet.

We enter into creation, and then for us it

becomes living. Things are dead in themselves ; only we give them life, and then, like fools, we turn around and are afraid of them, or enjoy them. But be not like certain fisherwomen, who, caught in a storm on their way home from market, took refuge in the house of a florist. They were lodged for the night in a room next the garden where the air was full of the fragrance of flowers. In vain did they try to rest, until one of their number suggested that they wet their fishy baskets and place them near their heads. Then they all fell into a sound sleep.

The world is our fish basket, we must not depend upon it for enjoyment. Those who do are the *tâmasas*, or the bound. Then there are the *râjasas*, or the egotistical, who talk always about "I," "I." They do good work sometimes and may become spiritual. But the highest are the *sâttvikas,* the introspective, those who live only in the Self. These three qualities, *tamas, rajas* and *sattva,* are in everyone, and different once predominate at different times.

Creation is not a "making" of something, it is the struggle to regain the equilibrium, as when atoms of cork are thrown to the bottom of a pail of water and rush to rise to the top, singly or in clusters. Life is and must be accompanied by evil. A little evil is the source of life ; the little wickedness that is in the world is very good, for when the balance is regained, the world will end, because sameness and destruction are one. When this world goes, good and evil go with it ; but when we can transcend this world we get rid of both good and evil and have bliss.

There is no possibility of ever having pleasure without pain, good without evil, for living itself is just the lost equilibrium. What we want is freedom, not life, nor pleasure, nor good. Creation is infinite, without beginning and without end, the ever-moving ripple in an infinite lake. There are yet unreached depths and others where the equilibrium has been regained, but the ripple is always progressing, the struggle to regain the balance is eternal. Life and death are only different names for the same fact, the two sides of the one coin. Both are *Mâyâ,* the inexplicable state of striving at one time to live, and a moment later to die. Beyond this is the true nature, the *A'tman.* While we recognize a God, it is really only the Self, from which we have separated ourselves and worship as outside of us; but it is our true Self all the time, the one and only God.

To regain the balance we must counteract *tamas* by *rajas,* then conquer *rajas* by *sattva,* the calm beautiful state that will grow and grow until all else is gone. Give up bondage, become a son, be free, and then you can "see the Father" as did Jesus. Infinite strength is religion and God. Avoid weakness and slavery. You are only a soul, *if* you are free; there is immortality for you, *if* you are free; there is a God, *if* He is free.

*   *   *   *   *

The world for me, not I for the world. Good and evil are our slaves, not we theirs. It is the nature of the brute to remain where he is (not to progress); it is the nature of man to seek good and avoid bad; it is the nature of God to seek neither, but just to be eternally blissful. Let us be gods! Make the heart like an ocean; go beyond all the trifles of the world; be mad with joy even at evil, see the world as a picture and then enjoy its beauty, knowing that nothing affects you. Children finding glass beads in a mud puddle, that is the good of the world. Look at it with calm complacency; see good and evil as the same, both are merely "Gods play"; enjoy all,

* * * * *

My Master used to say : " All is God, but tiger-God is to be shunned. All water is water, but we avoid dirty water for drinking."

The whole sky is the censer of God and the sun and moon are the lamps. What temple is needed ? All eyes are Thine, yet Thou hast not an eye ; all hands are Thine, yet Thou hast not a hand.

Neither seek nor avoid, take what comes. It is liberty to be affected by nothing ; do not merely endure, be unattached. Remember the story of the bull. A mosquito sat long on the horn of a certain bull ; then his conscience troubled him and he said : "Mr. Bull, I have been sitting here a long time, perhaps I annoy you. I am sorry, I will go away." But the bull replied : "Oh no, not at all ! Bring your whole family and live on my horn ; what can you do to me ?"

WEDNESDAY, *June 26th.*

Our best work is done, our greatest influence is exerted when we are without thought of self. All great geniuses know this. Let us open ourselves to the one Divine Actor and let Him act, and do nothing ourselves. "O Arjuna ! I have no duty in the whole world," says Krishna. Be perfectly resigned, perfectly unconcerned ; then alone can you do any true work. No eyes can see the real forces, we can only see the results. Put out self, lose it, forget it ; just let God work, it is His business. We have nothing to do but stand aside and let God work. The more we go away, the more

God comes in. Get rid of the little " I " and let only the great " I " live.

We are what our thoughts have made us, so take care of what you think. Words are secondary. Thoughts live, they travel far. Each thought we think is tinged with our own character, so that for the pure and holy man, even his jests or abuse will have the twist of his own love and purity and do good.

Desire nothing ; think of God and look for no return ; it is the desireless who bring results. The begging monks carry religion to every man's door ; but they think that they do nothing, they claim nothing, their work is unconsciously done. If they should eat of the tree of knowledge, they would become egoists and all the good they do would fly away. As soon as we say " I " we are humbugged all the time, and we call it " knowledge," but it is only going round and round like a bullock tied to a tree. The Lord has hidden Himself best and His work is best ; so he who hides himself best, accomplishes most. Conquer *yourself* and the whole universe is yours.

In the state of *sattva* we see the very nature of things, we go beyond the senses and beyond reason. The adamantine wall that shuts us in is egoism ; we refer everything to ourselves, thinking I do this, that and the other. Get rid of this puny "I" ; kill this diabolism in us ; "not I, but Thou," say it, feel it, live it. Until we give up the world manufactured by the ego, never can we enter the kingdom of heaven. None ever did, none ever will. To give up the world is to forget the ego, to know it not at all, living *in* the body, but not *of* it. This rascal ego must be obliterated. Bless men, when they revile you. Think how much good they are doing you ; they can only hurt themselves. Go where people hate you, let them thrash the ego out of you and you will get nearer to the Lord. Like the mother-monkey,* we hug our "baby," the world, as long as we can, but at last when we are driven to put it under our feet and step on it, then we are ready to come to God. Blessed it is to be persecuted for the sake of righteousness. Blessed are we if we cannot read, we have less to take us away from God.

Enjoyment is the million-headed serpent that we must tread under foot. We renounce, and go on, then find nothing and despair; but hold on, *hold on.* The world is a demon. It is a kingdom of which the puny ego is king. Put it away and stand firm. Give up lust and gold and fame and hold fast to the Lord, and at last we shall reach a state of perfect indiffer-

* The mother monkey is very fond of her young in time of safety; but when danger comes, she does not scruple to throw it down and trample on it, if necessary, to save herself. [Ed.]

ence. The idea that the gratification of the senses constitutes enjoyment is purely materialistic. There is not one spark of real enjoyment there: all the joy there is, is a mere reflection of the true bliss.

Those who give themselves up to the Lord do more for the world than all the so-called workers. One man who has purified himself thoroughly, accomplishes more than a regiment of preachers. *Out of purity and silence comes the word of power.*

"Be like a lily, stay in one place and expand your petals and the bees will come of themselves." There was a great contrast between Keshab Chunder Sen and Sri Râmakrishna. The second never recognized any sin or misery in the world, no evil to fight against. The first was a great ethical reformer, leader, and founder of the *Brâhmo-Samâj*. After twelve years the quiet prophet of Dakshineswar had worked a revolution not only in India, but in the world. The power is with the silent ones, who only live and love and then withdraw their personality. They never say "me" and "mine"; they are only blessed in being instruments. Such men are the makers of Christs and Buddhas, ever living, fully identified with God, ideal existences, asking nothing and not consciously doing anything. They are the real movers, the *Jivan-muktas,* absolutely selfless, the little personality entirely blown away, ambition non-existent. They are all principle, no personality.

THURSDAY, *June 27th (Swâmi brought the New Testament this morning and talked again on the book of John.)*

Mahommed claimed to be the "Comforter" that Christ promised to send. He considered it unnecessary to claim a supernatural birth for Jesus. Such claims have been common in all ages and in all countries. All great men have claimed gods for their fathers.

Knowing is only relative ; we can *be* God, but never *know* Him. Knowledge is a lower state ; Adam's fall was when he came to "know." Before that he was God, he was truth, he was purity. We are our own faces, but can see only a reflection, never the real thing. We are love, but when we think of it we have to use a phantasm, which proves that matter is only externalized thought.*

Nivritti is turning aside from the world. Hindu mythology says that the four first-

---

* Since the knower can know only his reflection and not himself, he is ever unknowable. So knowledge is distinct and separate from the knower, and as such it is externalized thought or thought standing outside the knower as a separate entity. Since the knower goes by the name of Spirit that which is distinct and separate from it should go by the name of Matter. Hence the Swâmi says " matter is only externalized thought."

created * were warned by a Swan (God Himself) that manifestation was only secondary, so they remained without creating. The meaning of this is that expression is degeneration, because spirit can only be expressed by the letter and then the "letter killeth"; † yet principle is bound to be clothed in matter, though we know that later we shall lose sight of the real in the covering. Every great teacher understands this and that is why a continual succession of prophets has to come to show us the principle and give it a new covering suited to the times. My Master taught that religion is one; all prophets teach the same, but they can only present the principle in a form, so they take it out of the old form and put it before us in a new one. When we free ourselves from name and form, especially from a body,—when we

---

* The four first-created were Sanaka, Sanandana, Sanâtana, and Sanatkumâra. [Ed.]

† Bible, 2 Cor. III., 6.

need no body, good or bad, then only do we escape from bondage. Eternal progression is eternal bondage; annihilation of form is to be preferred. We must get free from any body even a "god-body." God is the only real, existence, there cannot be two*. There is but One Soul and I am That.

Good works are only valuable as a means of escape; they do good to the doer, never to any other.

* * * *

Knowledge is mere classification. When we find many things of the same kind we call the sum of them by a certain name and are satisfied; we discover "facts," never "why." We take a circuit in a wider field of darkness and think we know something! No "why" can

* Body is a limitation. Hence the bodiless must be limitless or infinite. As there cannot be two Infinities, God or "One Soul" (who is bodiless) must be one and cannot be two.

be answered in this world, for that we must go to God. The Knower can never be expressed; it is as when a grain of salt drops into the ocean, it is at once merged in the ocean.

Differentiation creates; homogeneity or sameness is God. Get beyond differentiation; then you conquer life and death and reach eternal sameness and are in God, are God. Get freedom, even at the cost of life. All lives belong to us as leaves to a book; but we are unchanged, the Witness, the Soul, upon whom the impression is made, as when the impression of a circle is made upon the eyes when a firebrand is rapidly whirled round and round. The soul is the unity of all personalities, and because it is at rest, eternal, unchangeable, it is God, *Atman*. It is not life, but it is coined into life. It is not pleasure, but it is manufactured into pleasure.

*　　*　　*　　*

To-day God is being abandoned by the world

because He does not seem to be doing enough for the world, so they say, "Of what good is He?" Shall we look upon God as a mere municipal authority?

All we can do is to put down all desires, hates, differences; put down the lower self, commit mental suicide, as it were; keep the body and mind pure and healthy, but only as instruments to help us to God, that is their only true use. Seek truth for truth's sake alone, look not for bliss. It may come, but do not let that be your incentive. Have no motive except God. Dare to come to Truth even through hell.

FRIDAY, *June 28th.* (*The entire party went on a picnic for the day and although the Swâmi taught constantly, as he did wherever he was, no notes were taken and no record, therefore, of what he said remains. As he began his breakfast before setting out, however, he remarked;*)

Be thankful for all food, it is *Brahman*.* His universal energy is transmuted into our individual energy and helps us in all that we do.

SATURDAY, *June 29th*. (*The Swâmi came this morning with the* GITA *in his hand*.)

Krishna, the "Lord of souls," talks to Arjuna, or Gudâkesa, "lord of sleep" (he who has conquered sleep). The "field of virtue" (the battlefield) is this world ; the five brothers (representing righteousness) fight the hundred other brothers (all that we love and have to contend against) ; the most heroic brother, Arjuna (the awakened soul), is the general. We have to fight all sense-delights,

*Perhaps it will be well to explain here the difference between *Brahman* (neut.) and *Brahma'* (mas.). The former is the impersonal, beginningless supreme Self, the *Atman*. The latter is the first person of the Hindu Trinity(Brahmâ, Vishnu, Siva) and is the Creator of the Universe—(Ed.)

the things to which we are most attached, to kill them. We have to stand alone; we are *Brahman*, all other ideas must be merged into this one.

Krishna did everything but without any attachment; he was in the world, but not of it. "Do all work but without attachment; work for work's sake, never for yourself."

* * * * *

Freedom can never be true of name and form; it is the clay out of which we (the pots) are made; then it is limited and not free, so that freedom can never be true of the related. One pot can never say "I am free" as a pot; only as it loses all idea of form does it become free. The whole universe is only the Self with variations, the one tune made bearable by variation; sometimes there are discords, but they only make the subsequent harmony more perfect. In the universal melody three ideas stand out, freedom, strength and sameness.*

If your freedom hurts others, you are not free there ; you must not hurt others.

"To be weak is to be miserable," says Milton. Doing and suffering are inseparably joined. (Often, too, the man who laughs most is the one who suffers most.) "To work you have the right, not to the fruits thereof."

* * * * *

Evil thoughts, looked at materially, are the disease bacilli.

Each thought is a little hammer blow on the lump of iron which our bodies are, manufacturing out of it what we want it to be.

We are heirs to all the good thoughts of the universe, if we open ourselves to them.

The book is all in us. "Fool, hearest not thou? In thine own heart day and night is singing that Eternal Music,—*Satchidânanda*,

---

* These are the Swâmi's Trinity.

Soham, Soham. (Existence-Knowledge-Bliss Absolute, I am He, I am He.)

The fountain of all knowledge is in every one of us, in the ant as in the highest angel. Real religion is one, but we quarrel with the forms, the symbols, the illustrations. The millenium exists already for those who find it; we have lost ourselves and then think the world is lost.

Perfect strength will have no activity in this world; it only is, it does not act.

While real perfection is only one, relative perfections must be many.

SUNDAY, *June 30th.*

To try to think without a phantasm is to try to make the impossible possible. We cannot think "mammalia" without a concrete example, so with the idea of God.

The great abstraction of ideas in the world is what we call God.

Each thought has two parts,—the thinking and the word, and we must have both. Neither idealists nor materialists are right; we must take both idea and expression.

All knowledge is of the reflected, as we can only see our face in a mirror. No one will ever know his own Self or God, but we are that own Self, we are God.

In *Nirvâna* you are when *you* are not. Buddha said, "You are best, you are real when you are not." (When the little self is gone.)

The Light Divine within is obscured in most people. It is like a lamp in a cask of iron, no gleam of light can shine through. Gradually, by purity and unselfishness we can make the obscuring medium less and less dense, until at last it becomes as transparent as glass. Sri Râmakrishna was like the iron cask transformed into a glass cask, through which can be seen the inner light as it is. We are all on the way to become the cask of glass and even higher and higher reflections. As long as there is a "cask" at all, we must think through material means. No impatient one can ever succeed.

* * * *

Great saints are the object lessons of the Principle. But the disciples make the saint the Principle and then they forget the Principle in the person.

The result of Buddha's constant inveighing against a personal God was the introduction of idols into India. In the Vedas they knew them not because they saw God everywhere, but the reaction against the loss of God as Creator and Friend was to make idols, and Buddha became an idol—so too with Jesus. The range of idols is from wood and stone to Jesus and Buddha, but we must have idols.

* * * *

Violent attempts at reform always end by

retarding reform. Do not say "You are bad"; say only "You are good, but be better."

Priests are an evil in every country because they denounce and criticise, pulling at one string to mend it until two or three others are out of place. Love never denounces, only ambition does that. There is no such thing as "righteous" anger of justifiable killing.

If you do not allow one to become a lion, he will become a fox. Women are a power, only now it is more for evil because man oppresses her; she is the fox, but when she is no longer oppressed, she will become the lion.

Ordinarily speaking, spiritual aspiration ought to be balanced through the intellect, otherwise it may degenerate into mere sentimentality.

* * * *

All theists agree that behind the changeable there is an Unchangeable, though they vary in their conception of the Ultimate. Buddha denied this *in toto.* "There is no *Brahman*, no *Atman*, no soul" he said.

As a character Buddha was the greatest the world has ever seen; next to him Christ. But the teachings of Krishna as taught by the Gitâ are the grandest the world has ever known. He who wrote that wonderful poem was one of those rare souls whose lives send a wave of regeneration through the world. The human race will never again see such a brain as his who wrote the Gitâ.

*　　*　　*　　*

There is only one Power, whether manifesting as evil or good. God and the devil are the same river with the water flowing in opposite directions.

MONDAY, *July* 1*st.* (*Sri Râmakrishna Deva.*)

Sri Râmakrishna was the son of a very orthodox Bráhmin, who would refuse even a gift from any but a special caste of Brahmins; neither might he work, nor even be a priest in a temple, nor sell books nor serve anyone. He could only have " what fell from the skies" (alms) and even then it must not come through a "fallen" Brahmin. Temples have no hold on the Hindu religion; if they were all destroyed, religion would not be affected a grain. A man must only build a house for "God and guests," to build for himself would be selfish; therefore he erects temples as dwelling places for God.

Owing to the extreme poverty of his family, Sri Râmakrishna was obliged to become in his boyhood a priest in a temple dedicated to Divine Mother, also called *Prakriti* or *Kâli*, represented by a female figure standing with her feet on a male figure, indicating that until *Mâyâ* lifts, we can know nothing. *Brahman* is neuter, unknown and unknowable, but to be objectified he covers himself with a veil of *Mâyâ*, becomes the Mother of the Universe and so brings forth the creation. The prostrate figure (*Siva*, or God) has become *Sava* (dead, or lifeless) by being covered by *Mâyâ*. The *Jnâni* says "I will uncover God by force" (Advaitism); but the dualist says "we will uncover God by praying to Mother, begging Her to open the door to which She alone has the key."

The daily service of the Mother *Kâli* gradually awakened such intense devotion in the heart of the young priest that he could no longer carry on the regular temple worship, so he abandoned his duties and retired to a small woodland in the temple compound, where he gave himself up entirely to meditation. These woods were on the bank of the river Ganges and one day the swift current bore to his very feet just the necessary materials to build him a little hut. In this hut he stayed and wept and prayed, taking no thought for the care of his body or for aught except his Divine Mother. A relative fed him once a day and watched over him. Later came a girl *Sanyâsin* or ascetic, to help him find his "Mother." Whatever teachers he needed came to him unsought ; from every sect some holy saint would come and offer to teach him and to each he listened eagerly. But he worshipped only Mother ; all to him was Mother.

Sri Râmakrishna never spoke a harsh word against anyone. So beautifully tolerant was he that every sect thought that he belonged to them. He loved everyone. To him all religions were true. He found a place for each one. He was free, but free in love, not in "thunder." The mild type creates, the thundering type spreads. Paul was the thundering type to spread the light.*

* And it has been said by many that Swâmi Vivekânanda himself was a kind of St. Paul to Sri Râmakrishna. [Ed.]

The age of St. Paul, however, is gone; we are to be the new lights for this day. A self-adjusting organization is the great need of our time. When we can get one, that will be the last religion of the world. The wheel must turn, and we should help it, not hinder. The waves of religious thought rise and fall and on the topmost one stands the "prophet of the period." Râmakrishna came to teach the religion of today, constructive, not destructive. He had to go afresh to Nature to ask for facts and he got scientific religion, which never says "believe," but "see"; "I see, and you too can see." Use the same means and you will reach the same vision. God will come to everyone, harmony is within the reach of all. Sri Râmakrishna's teachings are "the gist of Hinduism;" they were not peculiar to him. Nor did he claim that they were; he cared naught for name or fame.

He began to preach when he was about forty; but he never went out to do it. He waited for those who wanted his teachings to come to him. In accordance with Hindu custom, he was married by his parents in early youth to a little girl of five, who remained at home with her family in a distant village, unconscious of the great struggle through which her young husband was passing. When she reached maturity, he was already deeply absorbed in religious devotion. She travelled on foot from her home to the temple at Dakshineswara where he was then living, and as soon as she saw him she recognized what he was, for she herself was a great soul, pure and holy, who only desired to help his work and never to drag him down to the level of the *grihastha* (householder).

Sri Râmakrishna is worshipped in India as one of the great Incarnations and his birthday is celebrated there as a religious festival.

* * * *

A curious round stone is the emblem of Vishnu, the omnipresent. Each morning a priest comes in, offers sacrifice to the idol, waves incense before him, then puts him to bed and apologizes to God for worshipping him in that way, because he can only conceive of him through an image or by means of some material object. He bathes the idol, clothes him, and puts his divine self into the idol "to make it alive."

* * * *

There is a sect which says: "It is weakness to worship only the good and beautiful, we ought also to love and worship the hideous and the evil." This sect prevails all over Thibet and they have no marriage. In India proper they cannot exist openly, but organize secret societies. No decent men will belong to them except *sub rosa.* Thrice communism was tried in Thibet and thrice it failed. They use *tapas* and with immense success as far as power is concerned.

Tapas means literally "to burn." It is a kind of penance to "heat" the higher nature. It is sometimes in the form of a sunrise to sunset vow, such as repeating *Om* all day incessantly. These actions will produce a certain power that you can convert into any form you wish, spiritual or material. This idea of *tapas* penetrates the whole of Hindu religion. The Hindus even say that God made *tapas* to create the world. It is a mental instrument with which to do everything. "Everything in the three worlds can be caught by *tapas.*"

* * * *

People who report about sects with which they are not in sympathy are both conscious and unconscious liars. A believer in one sect can rarely see truth in others.

* * * * *

A great Bhakta (Hanumân) once said when asked what day of the month it was," God is my eternal date, no other date I care for."

TUESDAY, *July 2nd (The Divine Mother.)* *Sâktas* worship the Universal Energy as Mother, the sweetest name they know; for the mother is the highest ideal of womanhood in India. When God is worshipped as "Mother," as Love, the Hindus call it the" right-handed" way and it leads to spirituality, but never to material prosperity. When God is worshipped on His terrible side, that is, in the"left-handed" way, it leads usually to great material prosperity, but rarely to spirituality; and eventually it leads to degeneration and the obliteration of the race who practise it.

Mother is the first manifestation of power and is considered a higher idea than father. With the name of mother comes the idea of *Sakti*, Divine Energy and omnipotence, just as the baby believes its mother to be all-powerful, able to do anything. The Divine Mother is the *Kundalini* sleeping in us, without worshipping Her we can never know ourselves. All-merciful, all-powerful, omnipresent are attributes of Divine Mother. She is the sum-total of the energy in the universe. Every manifestation of power in the universe is "Mother." She is Life, She is Intelligence, She is Love. She is in the universe, yet separate from it. She is a person and can be seen and known (as Sri Râmakrishna saw and new Her). Established in the idea of Mother we can do anything. She quickly answers prayer.

She can show Herself to us in any form at any moment. Divine Mother can have form (*rupa*) and name (*nâma*), or name without form, and as we worship Her in these various aspects we can rise to pure Being, having neither form nor name.

The sum-total of all the cells in an organism is one person, so each soul is like one cell and the sum of them is God, and beyond that is the Absolute. The sea calm is the Absolute; the same sea in waves is Divine Mother. She is time, space and causation. God is Mother and has two natures, the conditioned and the unconditioned. As the former, She is God, Nature and soul (man). As the latter, She is unknown and unknowable. Out of the Unconditioned came the trinity, God, Nature and soul, the triangle of existence. This is the Visishtâdvaitist idea.

A bit of Mother, a drop, was Krishna, another was Buddha, another was Christ. The worship of even one spark of Mother in our earthly mother leads to greatness. Worship Her if you want love and wisdom.

WEDNESDAY, *July 3rd.*

Generally speaking, human religion begins with fear. "The fear of the Lord is the beginning of wisdom." But later comes the higher idea "Perfect love casteth out fear." Traces of fear will remain with us until we get knowledge, know what God is. Christ, being man had to see impurity and denounced it; but God infinitely higher, does not see iniquity and cannot be angry. Denunciation is never the highest, David's hands were smeared with blood; he could not build the temple.

The more we grow in love and virtue and holiness, the more we see love and virtue and holiness outside. All condemnation of others really condemns ourselves. Adjust the microcosm (which is in your power to do) and the macrocosm will adjust itself for you. It is like the hydrostatic paradox, one drop of water can balance the universe. We cannot see outside what we are not inside. The universe is to us what the huge engine is to the miniature engine; an indication of any error in the tiny engine leads us to imagine trouble in the huge one.

Every step that has been really gained in the world has been gained by love; criticising can never do any good, it has been tried for thousands of years. Condemnation accomplishes nothing.

A real Vedântist must sympathize with all. Monism or absolute oneness is the very soul of Vedânta. Dualists naturally tend to become intolerant, to think theirs the only way. The *Vaishnavas* in India, who are dualists, are a most intolerant sect. Among the *Saivas,* another dualistic sect, the story is told of a devotee by the name of Ghanta-karna, or the Bell.eared, who was so devout a worshipper of Siva that he did not wish even to hear the name of any other deity, so he wore two bells tied to his ears in order to drown the sound of any voice uttering other Divine names. On account of his intense devotion to Siva the latter wanted to teach him that there was no difference between Siva and Vishnu, so he appeared before him as half Vishnu and half Siva. At that moment the devotee was waving incense before him, but so great was the bigotry of Ghantakarna that when he saw the fragrance of the incense entering the nostril of Vishnu, he thrust his finger into it to prevent the god from enjoying the sweet smell.

* * * *

The meat-eating animal, like the lion, gives

one blow and subsides, but the patient bullock goes on all day, eating and sleeping as it walks. The "live Yankee" cannot compete with the rice-eating Chinese coolie. While military power dominates, meat-eating will prevail; but with the advance of science fighting will grow less and then the vegetarians will come in.

*   *   *   *

We divide ourselves into two to love God,—myself loving my Self. God has created me and I have created God. We create God in our image; it is we who create Him to be our master, it is not God who makes us His servants. When we know that we are one with God, that we and He are friends, then come equality and freedom. So long as you hold yourself separated by a hair's breadth from this Eternal One, fear cannot go.

Never ask that foolish question, what good will it do to the world? Let the world go.

Love and ask nothing ; love and look for nothing further. Love and forget all the "isms." Drink the cup of love and become mad. Say "Thine, O Thine forever O Lord !" and plunge in, forgetting all else. The very idea of God is love. Seeing a cat loving her kittens, stand and pray. God has become manifest there ; literally believe this. Repeat "I am Thine, I am Thine", for we can see God everywhere. Do not seek for Him, just see Him.

"May the Lord ever keep you alive, light of the world, soul of the universe !"

*　　*　　*　　*

The Absolute cannot be worshipped, so we must worship a manifestation, such a one as has our nature. Jesus had our nature ; he became the Christ ; so can we and so *must* we. Christ and Buddha were the names of a state to be attained; Jesus and Gautama were the persons to manifest it. "Mother" is the first and highest manifestation, next the Christs and Buddhas. We make our own environment and we strike the fetters off. The *Atman* is the fearless. When we pray to a God, outside it is good, only we do not know what we do. When we know the Self, we understand. The highest expression of love is unification.

"There was a time when I was a woman and he was a man,
Still love grew until there was neither he nor I;
Only I remember faintly there was a time when there were two,
But love came between and made them one."

(Persian Sufi Poem).

Knowledge exists eternally and is co-existent with God. The man who discovers a spiritual law is inspired and what he brings is revelation, but revelation too is eternal, not to be crystallized as final and then blindly followed. The Hindus have been criticised so many years by their conquerors that they (the Hindus) dare to criticise their religion themselves, and this makes them free. Their foreign rulers struck off their fetters without knowing it. The most religious people on earth, the Hindus have actually no sense of blasphemy; to speak of holy things in any way is to them in itself a sanctification. Nor have they any artificial respect for prophets or books, or for hypocritical piety.

The Church tries to fit Christ into it, not the Church into Christ; so only those writings were preserved that suited the purpose in hand. Thus the books are not to be depended upon and book-worship is the worst kind of idolatry to bind our feet. All has to conform to the book,—science, religion, philosophy;

it is the most horrible tyranny, this tyranny of the Protestant Bible. Every man in Christian countries has a huge cathedral on his head, and on top of that a Book, and yet man lives and grows ! Does not this prove that man is God ?

Man is the highest being that exists and this is the greatest world. We can have no conception of God higher than man, so our God is man and man is God. When we rise and go beyond and find something higher, we have to jump out of the mind, out of body and the imagination and leave this world ; when we rise to be the Absolute, we are no longer in this world. Man is the apex of the only world we can ever know. All we know of animals is only by analogy, we judge them by what we do and feel ourselves.

The sum-total of knowledge is ever the same,

only sometimes it is more manifested and sometimes less. The only source of it is within and there only is it found.

* * * *

All poetry, painting and music is feeling expressed through words, through color, through sound.

* * * *

Blessed are those upon whom their sins are quickly visited, their account is the sooner balanced ! Woe to those whose punishment is deferred, it is the greater !

Those who have attained sameness are said to be living in God. All hatred is killing the "Self by the self," therefore love is the law of life. To rise to this is to be perfect, but the more perfect we are, the less work (so-called) can we do. The *sâttvikas* see and know that all is mere child's play and do not trouble themselves about anything.

It is easy to strike a blow, but tremendously hard to stay the hand, stand still and say : " In Thee O Lord I take refuge," and then wait for Him to act.

FRIDAY, *July 5th.*

Until you are ready to change any minute you can never see the truth ; but you must, hold fast and be steady in the search for truth.

* * * *

Chârvâkas, a very ancient sect in India, were rank materialists. They have died out now and most of their books are lost. They claimed that the soul, being the product of the body and its forces, died with it ; that there was no proof of its further existence. They denied inferential knowledge, accepting only perception by the senses.

* * * *

Samâdhi is when the Divine and human are in one, or it is "bringing sameness."

* * * *

Materialism says, The voice of freedom is a delusion. Idealism says, The voice that tells of bondage is delusion. Vedânta says, You are free and not free at the same time ; never free on the earthly plane, but ever free on the spiritual.

Be beyond both freedom and bondage.

We are *Siva*, we are immortal knowledge beyond the senses.

Infinite power is back of everyone ; pray to "Mother" and it will come to you.

" O Mother, giver of *Vâk* (eloquence), Thou self-existent, come as the *Vâk* upon my lips." (Hindu invocation).

" That Mother whose voice is in the thunder, come Thou in me ! *Kâli*, Thou time eternal, Thou force irresistible, *Sakti*, Power !"

SATURDAY, *July 6th.* (*To-day we had Sankarâcharya's commentary on Vyâsa's Vedânta Sutras*)

Om taṭ sat !

According to Sankara, there are two phases of the universe, one is I and the other thou; and they are as contrary as light and darkness, so it goes without saying that neither can be derived from the other. On the subject, the object has been superimposed; the subject is the only reality, the other a mere appearance. The opposite view is untenable. Matter and the external world are but the soul in a certain state; in reality there is only one.

All our world comes from truth and untruth coupled together. *Samsâra* (life) is the result of the contradictory forces acting upon us, like the diagonal motion of a ball in a parallelogram of forces. The world is God and is real, but that is not the world we see; just as we see silver in the mother-of-pearl where it is not.

This is what is known as *Adhyâsa* or superimposition, that is, a relative existence dependent upon a real one, as when we recall a scene we have seen; for the time it exists for us, but that existence is not real. Or some say, it is as when we imagine heat in water, which does not belong to it; so really it is something which has been put where it does not belong, "taking the thing for what it is not." We see reality, but distorted by the medium through which we see it.

You can never know yourself except as objectified. When we mistake one thing for another, we always take the thing before us as the real, never the unseen; thus we mistake the object for the subject. The *Atman* never becomes the object. Mind is the internal sense the outer senses are its instruments. In the subject is a trifle of the objectifying power that enables him to know "I am"; but the subject is the object of its own self, never of the mind or the senses. You can, however, superimpose one idea on another idea, as when we say "the sky is blue", the sky itself being only an idea.

Science and nescience are all there are, but the Self is never affected by any nescience. Relative knowledge is good, because it leads to absolute knowledge; but neither the knowledge of the senses, nor of the mind, nor even of the Vedas is true, since they are all within the realm of relative knowledge. First get rid of the delusion "I am the body", then only can we want real knowledge. Man's knowledge is only a higher degree of brute knowledge.

* * * *

One part of the Vedas deals with *Karma*,—forms and ceremonies. The other part deals with the knowledge of *Brahman* and discusses religion. The Vedas in this part teach of the Self and because they do, their knowledge is approaching real knowledge. Knowledge of the Absolute depends upon no book, nor upon anything; it is absolute in itself. No amount of study will give this knowledge; it is not theory, it is realization. Cleanse the dust from the mirror, purify your own mind, and in a flash you know that you are *Brahman.*

God exists, not birth or death, not pain, nor misery, nor murder, nor change, nor good or evil; all is *Brahman.* We take the "rope for the serpent," the error is ours...We can only do good when we love God and He reflects our love. The murderer is God and the "clothing of murderer" is only superimposed upon him. Take him by the hand and tell him the truth.

Soul has no caste and to think it has is a delusion, so are life and death or any motion or quality. The *Atman* never changes, never goes or comes. It is the eternal Witness of all its own manifestations, but we take it for the manifestation; an eternal illusion, without beginning or end, ever going on. The Vedas, however, have to come down to our level, for if they told us the highest truth in the highest way, we could not understand it.

Heaven is a mere superstition arising from desire, and desire is ever a yoke, a degeneration. Never approach anything except as God; for if we do, we see evil; because we throw a veil of delusion over what we look at and then we see evil. Get free from these illusions; be blessed. Freedom is to lose all illusions.

In one sense *Brahman* is known to every human being; he knows "I am"; but man does not know himself *as* he is. We all know we are, but not how we are. All lower explanations are partial truths; but the flower, the essence of the Vedas is that the

Self in each of us is *Brahman*. Every phenomenon is included in birth, growth and death; appearance, continuance and disappearance. Our own realization is beyond the Vedas, because even they depend upon that. The highest Vedânta is the philosophy of the Beyond.

To say that creation has any beginning is to lay the axe at the root of all philosophy.

Mâyâ is the energy of the universe, potential and kinetic. Until Mother releases us, we cannot get free.

The universe is ours to enjoy, but want nothing. To want is weakness. Want makes us beggars and we are sons of the king, not beggars.

SUNDAY MORNING, *July 7th*.

Infinite manifestation dividing itself in portions

still remains infinite, and each portion is infinite.*

Brahman is the same in two forms,—changeable and unchangeable, expressed and unexpressed. Know that the Knower and the known are one. The Trinity, the Knower, the known and knowing, is manifesting as this universe. That God the *Yogi* sees in meditation, he sees through the power of his own Self.

What we call nature, fate, is simply God's will.

So long as enjoyment is sought, bondage remains. Only imperfection can enjoy, because enjoyment is the fulfilling of desire. The human soul enjoys Nature. The underlying reality of Nature, soul and God is *Brahman*; but it (Brahman) is unseen, until we bring it

* Infinity is one, without a second, ever indivisible, and unmanifested. By 'infinite manifestation,' the Swâmi means the universe, both visible and invisible. Although it is made up of countless forms which are limited by their very nature, still as a whole it is always infinite ; nay even a portion of it is infinite, as each such portion is inseparably united with it.

out. It may be brought out by *Pramantha* or friction, just as we can produce fire by friction. The body is the lower piece of wood, *Om* is the pointed piece and *dhyâna* (meditation) is the friction. When this is used, that light which is the knowledge of *Brahman* will burst forth in the soul. Seek it through *tapas*. Holding the body upright, sacrifice the organs of sense in the mind. The sense-centres are within, the organs without, so drive them into the mind and through *dhârana* (concentration) fix the mind in *dhyâna*. *Brahman* is omnipresent in the universe as is butter in milk, but friction makes it manifest in one place. As churning brings out the butter in the milk, so *dhyâna* brings the realization of *Brahman* in the soul.

All Hindu philosophy declares that there is a sixth sense, the superconscious, and through it comes inspiration.

* * * *

The universe is motion, and friction will eventually bring everything to an end; then comes a rest and after that all begins again.

* * * *

So long as the "skin sky" surrounds man, that is, so long as he identifies himself with his body, he cannot see God.

SUNDAY AFTERNOON.

There are six schools of philosophy in India that are regarded as orthodox because they believe in the Vedas.

Vyâsa's philosophy is *par excellence* that of the Upanishads. He wrote in Sutra form, that is in brief algebraical symbols without nominative or verb. This caused so much ambiguity that out of the *Sutras* came dualism, mono-dualism, and monism or "roaring Vedânta"; and all the great commentators in these different schools were at times "conscious liars" in order to make the texts suit their philosophy.

The Upanishads contain very little history of the doings of any man, but nearly all other Scriptures are largely personal histories. The Vedas deal almost entirely with philosophy. Religion without philosophy runs into superstition; philosophy without religion becomes dry atheism.

Visishta-advaita is qualified *advaita* (monism). Its expounder was Râmânuja. He says, "Out of the ocean of milk of the Vedas Vyâsa has churned this butter of philosophy, the better to help mankind." He says again, "All virtues and all qualities belong to Brahmâ, Lord of the universe. He is the greatest *Purusha* and *Brahman* (neut.) is lower, or the universe itself." Madhva is a thorough-going dualist or dvaitist. He claims that every caste and even women might study the Vedas. He quotes chiefly from the *Purânas*. He says that *Brahman* means Vishnu, not Siva at all, because there is no salvation except through Vishnu.

MONDAY, *July 8th.*

There is no place for reasoning in Madhva's explanation, it is all taken from the revelation in the Vedas.

Râmânuja says, the Vedas are the holiest study. Let the sons of the three upper castes get the Sutras and at eight, ten, or eleven years of age begin the study, which means going to a *Guru* and learning the Vedas word for word, with perfect intonation and pronunciation.

Japa is repeating the Holy Name; through this the devotee rises to the Infinite. The boat of sacrifice and ceremonies is very frail, we need more than that to know *Brahman*, which alone is freedom. Liberty is nothing more than destruction of ignorance and that can only go when we know *Brahman*. It is not necessary to go through all these ceremonials to reach the meaning of the Vedânta. Repeating *Om* is enough.

Seeing difference is the cause of all misery, and ignorance is the cause of seeing difference. That is why ceremonials are not needed, because they increase the idea of inequality ; you practise them to get rid of something, or to obtain something.

Brahman is without action, *Atman* is *Brahman* and we are *Atman* ; knowledge like this takes off all error. It must be heard, apprehended intellectually, and lastly realized. Cogitating is applying reason and establishing this knowledge in ourselves by reason. Realizing is making it a part of our lives by constant thinking of it. This constant thought or *dhyânam* is as oil that pours in one unbroken line from vessel to vessel ; *dhyânam* rolls the mind in this thought day and night and so helps us to attain to liberation. Think always "*Soham, Soham*"; this is almost as good as liberation. Say it day and night; realization will come as the result of this continuous cogitation. This absolute and continuous remembrance of the Lord is what is meant by *Bhakti*.

This *Bhakti* is indirectly helped by all good works. Good thoughts and good works create less differentiation than bad ones, so indirectly they lead to freedom. Work, but give up the results to the Lord. Knowledge alone can make us perfect. He who follows the God of Truth with devotion, to him the God of Truth reveals Himself.

* * * *

We are lamps and our burning is what we call "life." When the supply of oxygen gives out, then the lamp must go out. All we can do is to keep the lamp clean. Life is a product, a compound, and as such must resolve itself into its elements.

TUESDAY, *July 9th.*

Man as *Atman* is really free, as man he is bound, changed by every physical condition. As man, he is a machine with an idea of freedom; but this human body is the best and the human mind the highest mind there is. When a man attains to the *Atman* state he can take a body, making it to suit himself; he is above law. This is a statement and must be proved. Each one must prove it for himself; we may satisfy ourselves but we cannot satisfy another. *Râja Yoga* is the only science of religion that can be demonstrated, and only what I myself have proved by experience, do I teach. The full ripeness of reason is intuition, but intuition cannot antagonize reason.

Work purifies the heart and so leads to *vidyâ* (wisdom). The Buddhists said doing good to men and to animals were the only works; the Brahmins said that worship and all ceremonials were equally "work" and purify the mind. Sankara declares that "all works, good and bad, are against knowledge." Actions tending to ignorance are sins, not directly, but as causes, because they tend to increase *tamas* and *rajas*. With *sattva* only, comes wisdom. Virtuous deeds take off the veil from knowledge and knowledge alone can make us see God.

Knowledge can never be created, it can only be discovered; and every man who makes a great discovery is inspired. Only, when it is a spiritual truth he brings, we call him a prophet; and when it is on the physical plane, we call him a scientific man and we attribute more importance to the former, although the source of all truth is One.

Sankara says *Brahman* is the essence, the reality of all knowledge and that all manifestation as Knower, knowing and known are mere imaginings in *Brahman.* Râmânuja attributes consciousness to God; the real monists attribute nothing, not even existence in any meaning that we can attach to it. Râmânuja declares that God is the essence of conscious knowledge. Undifferentiated consciousness, when differentiated, becomes the world.

* * * *

Buddhism, one of the most philosophical religions in the world, spread all through the populace, the common people of India. What a wonderful culture there must have been among the Aryans twenty-five hundred years ago, to be able to grasp such ideas!

Buddha was the only great Indian philosopher who would not recognise caste, and not one of his followers remains in India. All the other philosophers pandered more or less to social prejudices ; no matter how high they soared, still a bit of the vulture remained in them. As my Master used to say, "The vulture soars high out of sight in the sky, but his eye is ever on a bit of carrion on the earth."

* * * *

The ancient Hindus were wonderful scholars, veritable living encyclopædias. They said, "knowledge in books and money in other people's hands is like no money and no knowledge at all."

Sankara was regarded by many as an incarnation of Siva.

WEDNESDAY, *July* 10*th*.

There are sixty-five million Mohammedans in India, most of them *Sufis.** *Sufis* identify

* The influence of Hinduism upon Mahommedanism in India gave rise to the sect known as *Sufis* or *Shias.* [Ed.]

man with God and through them this idea came into Europe. They are also called " *Shias.*" They say " I am that Truth "; but they have an esoteric as well as an exoteric doctrine, although Mohammed himself did not hold it.

"Hashshashin"* has become our word "assassin", because the old sects of Mohammedanism killed non-believers as a part of their creed.

A pitcher of water has to be present in the Mohammedan worship as a symbol of God filling the universe.

* * * *

The Hindus believe that there will be ten

* The name of a military and religious order existing in Syria in the 11th century and famous for the number of secret murders committed by its members in obedience to the will of their chief. The literal meaning of the word is " Hashish-eater " and was applied to the order because of their habitual use of this special drug to fortify the murderers for their task. [Ed.]

Divine Incarnations. Nine have been and the tenth is still to come.

* * * *

Sankara sometimes resorts to sophistry in order to prove that the ideas in the Books go to uphold his philosophy. Buddha was more brave and sincere than any teacher. He said : "Believe no book ; Vedas* are all humbug. If they agree with me, so much the better for the books. I am the greatest book ; sacrifice and prayer are useless." Buddha was the first human being to give to the world a complete system of morality. He was good for good's sake, he loved for love's sake.

Sankara says: God is to be reasoned on, because the Vedas say so. Reason helps inspiration ; books and realized reason,—or individualized perception—both are proofs of God. The Vedas are, according to him, a sort

*By Vedas is here meant the *Karma-Kanda* or first portion.

of incarnation of universal knowledge. The proof of God is that he brought forth the Vedas, and the proof of the Vedas is that such wonderful books could only have been given out by *Brahman*. They are the mine of all knowledge and they have come out of Him as a man breathes out air; therefore we know that He is infinite in power and knowledge. He may or may not have created the world, that is a trifle; to have produced the Vedas is more important! The world has come to know God through the Vedas; no other way there is.

And so universal is this belief, held by Sankara, in the all-inclusiveness of the Vedas that there is even a Hindu proverb that if a man loses his cow, he goes to look for her in the Vedas!

Sankara further affirms that obedience to ceremonial is not knowledge. Knowledge of

God is independent of moral duties, or sacrifice, or ceremonial, or what we think or do not think, just as the stump is not affected when one man takes it for a ghost and another sees it as it is.

Vedânta is necessary because neither reasoning nor books can show us God. He is only to be realized by superconscious perception and Vedânta teaches how to attain that. You must get beyond personal God (*Isvara*) and reach the Absolute *Brahman*. God is the perception of every being ; He is all there is to be perceived. That which says " I " is *Brahman*, but although we, day and night, perceive Him, we do not know that we are perceiving Him. As soon as we become aware of this truth, all misery goes ; so we must get knowledge of the truth. Reach unity ; no more duality will come. But knowledge does not come by sacrifice, but by seeking, worshipping, knowing the *Atman*.

Brahmavidyâ is the highest knowledge, knowing the *Brahman* ; lower knowledge is science. This is the teaching of the *Mundakopanishad,* or the Upanishad for *Sanyâsins.* There are two sorts of knowledge,—principal and secondary. The unessential is that part of the Vedas dealing with worship and ceremonial, also all secular knowledge. The essential is that by which we reach the Absolute. It (the Absolute) creates all from its own nature ; there is nothing to cause, nothing outside. It is all energy, it is all there is. He who makes all sacrifices to himself, the *Atman,* he alone knows *Brahman.* Fools think outside worship the highest ; fools think works can give us God. Only those whe go through the *Susumna* (the "path" of the *Yogis*) reach the *Atman.* They must go to a *Guru* to learn. Each part has the same nature as the whole ; all springs from the *Atman.* Meditation is the arrow, the whole soul going out to God is the bow, which speeds the arrow to its mark, the *Atman*. As finite we can never express the Infinite, but we are the Infinite. Knowing this we argue with no one.

Divine wisdom is to be got by devotion, meditation and chastity. "Truth alone triumphs, and not untruth." Through truth alone the way is spread to Brahman, where alone love and truth are.

THURSDAY, *July* 11*th*.

Without mother-love no creation could continue. Nothing is entirely physical, nor yet entirely metaphysical; one presupposes the other and explains the other. All Theists agree that there is a background to this visible universe, they differ as to the nature or character of that background. Materialists say there is no background.

In all religions the superconscious state is identical. Hindus, Christians, Mohammedans, Buddhists, and even those of no creed, all have the very same experience when they transcend the body.

*   *   *   *

The purest Christians in the world were established in India by the Apostle Thomas about twenty-five years after the death of Jesus. This was while the Anglo-Saxons were still savages, painting their bodies and living in caves. The Christians in India once numbered about three millions, but now there are about one million.

Christianity is always propagated by the sword. How wonderful that the disciples of such a gentle soul should kill so much! The three missionary religions are the Buddhist, Mohammedan and Christian. The three older ones, Hinduism, Judaism and Zoroastrianism, never sought to make converts. Buddhists never killed, but converted three-quarters of the world at one time by pure gentleness.

The Buddhists were the most logical agnostics. You can really stop nowhere between nihilism and absolutism. The Buddhists were intellectually all-destroyers, carrying their theory to its ultimate logical issue. The Advaitists also worked out their theory to its logical conclusion and reached the Absolute, one identified Unit Substance, out of which all phenomena are being manifested. Both Buddhists and Advaitists have a feeling of identity and non-identity at the same time; one of these feelings must be false and one true. The nihilist puts the reality in non-identity, the realist puts the reality in identity; and this is the fight which occupies the whole world. This is the "tug of war."

The realist asks, "How does the nihilist get any idea of identity?" How does the revolving light appear a circle? A point of rest alone explains motion. The nihilist can never explain the genesis of the delusion that there is a background; neither can the idealist explain how the One becomes the many. The only explanation must come from beyond the sense-plane; we must rise to the superconscious, to a state entirely beyond sense perception. That metaphysical power is the further instrument that the idealist alone can use. He can experience the Absolute; the man Vivekânanda can resolve himself into the Absolute and then come back to the man again. For him, then, the problem is solved and secondarily for others, for he can show the way to others. Thus religion begins where philosophy ends. The "good to the world" will be that what is now superconscious for us will in ages to come be the conscious for all. Religion is therefore the highest work the world has; and because man has unconsciously felt this, he has clung through all the ages to the idea of religion.

Religion the great milch cow has given many kicks, but never mind, it gives a great deal of milk. The milkman does not mind the kick of the cow which gives much milk. Religion is the greatest child to be born, the great "moon of realization," let us feed it and help it grow and it will become a giant. King Desire and King Knowledge fought and just as the latter was about to be defeated, a child was born to him, Vedânta, and saved the victory to him. Then Love (*Bhakti*) and Knowledge married and "lived happy ever after." Love concentrates all the power of the will without effort, as when a man falls in love with a woman.

The path of devotion is natural and pleasant. Philosophy is taking the mountain stream back to its source by force. It is a quicker method but very hard. Philosophy says, "check everything." Devotion says, "give up all to the stream, have eternal self-surrender." It is a longer way, but easier and happier.

"Thine am I forever; henceforth whatever I do, it is Thou doing it. No more is there any me or mine."

"Having no money to give, no brains to learn, no time to practice Yoga, to Thee, O sweet One, I give myself, to Thee my body and mind."

No amount of ignorance or wrong ideas can put a barrier between the soul aud God. Even if there be no God, still hold fast to love. It is better to die seeking a God than as a dog seeking only carrion. Chose the highest ideal and give your life up to that. Death being so certain, it is the highest thing to give up life for a great purpose.

Love will painlessly attain to philosophy; then after knowledge comes *Parâbhakti* (supreme devotion).

Knowledge is critical and makes a great fuss over everything; but Love says "God will show His real nature to me" and accepts all.

RABBIA.

Rabbia, sick upon her bed,
By two saints was visited,—

Holy Malik, Hassan wise,
Men of mark in Moslem eyes.

Hassan said, "Whose prayer is pure,
Will God's chastisements endure."

Malik, from a deeper sense
Uttered his experience :—

"He who loves his master's choice
Will in chastisement *rejoice*."

Rabbia saw some selfish will
In their maxims lingering still,

And replied; "O men of grace,
He who sees his Master's face

Will not in his prayers recall
That he is chastised at all!"

Persian Poem.

FRIDAY, *July* 12*th*. (*Sankara's Commentary*).

Fourth Vyâsa *Sutra*: "*Atman* (is) the aim of all."

The *Isvara* is to be known from the Vedânta; all Vedas point to Him (who is the Cause; the Creator, Preserver and Destroyer). *Isvara* is the unification of the Trinity, known as Brahmâ Vishnu and Siva, which stands at the head of the Hindu Pantheon. "Thou art our Father who takest us to the other shore of the dark ocean." (Invocation to *Isvara*).

The Vedas cannot show you *Brahman*, you are That already ; they can only help to take away the veil that hides the truth from our eyes. The first veil to vanish is ignorance, and when that is gone, sin goes, next desire ceases, selfishness ends and all misery disappears. This cessation of ignorance can only come when I know that God and I are one ; in other words, identify yourself with *Atman*, not with human limitations. *Dis*-identify yourself with the body and all pain will cease. This is the secret of healing. The universe is a case of hypnotization ; de-hypnotize yourself and cease to suffer.

In order to be free we have to pass through vice to virtue, and then get rid of both. *Tamas* is to be conquered by *rajas*, both are to be submerged in *sattva* ; then, go beyond the three qualities. Reach a state where your very breathing is a prayer.

Whenever you learn (gain anything) from another man's words, know that you had the experience in a previous existence, because experience is the only teacher. *

With all powers comes further misery, so kill desire. Getting any desire is like putting a stick into a nest of hornets. *Vairâgyam* is finding out that desires are but gilded balls of poison.

" Mind is not God " (Sankara). "*Tat tvam asi*," "*Aham Brahmasmi*" (" That thou art," " I am *Brahman* "). When a man realizes this, all the knots of his heart are cut asunder, all his doubts vanish. Fearlessness is not possible

---

* Whenever you know any person, place or thing, you know it because you can remember it ; if you cannot, you say that you do not know it, and you can only remember that which you experienced before. So experience is the only teacher.

as long as we have even God *over* us ; we must *be* God. What is disjoined will be forever disjoined ; if you are separate from God, then you can never be one with Him, and *vice versa.* If by virtue you are joined to God, when that ceases, disjunction will come. The junction is eternal and virtue only helps to remove the veil. We are *âzâd* (free), we must realize it. "Whom the Self chooses" means we are the Self and choose ourselves.

Does seeing depend upon our own efforts or does it depend upon something outside ? It depends upon ourselves ; our efforts take off the dust, the mirror does not change. There is neither knower, knowing nor known. "He who knows that he does not know, he knows It." He who has a theory knows nothing.

The idea that we are bound is only an illusion.

Religion is not of this world; it is "heart-cleansing" and its effect on this world is secondary. Freedom is inseparable from the nature of the *Atman*. This is ever pure, ever perfect, ever unchangeable. This *Atman* you can never know. We can say nothing about the *Atman* but "not this, not this."

"*Brahman* is that which we can never drive out by any power of mind or imagination." (Sankara).

* * * *

The universe is thought, and the Vedas are the words of this thought. We can create and uncreate this whole universe. Repeating the words, the unseen thought is aroused and as a result a seen effect is produced. This is the claim of a certain sect of *Karmis*. They think that each one of us is a creator. Pronounce the words, the thought which corresponds will arise and the result will become visible. "Thought is the power of the word, the word is the expression of the thought," say the *Mimânsakas*, a Hindu philosophical sect.

SATURDAY, *July 13th.*

Everything we know is a compound and all sense-knowledge comes through analysis. To think that mind is a simple, single or independent, is dualism. Philosophy is not got by studying books; the more you read books, the more muddled becomes the mind. The idea of unthinking philosophers was that the mind was a simple, and this led them to believe in free-will. Psychology, the analysis of the mind, shows the mind to be a compound, and every compound must be held together by some outside force; so the will is bound by the combination of outside forces. Man cannot even will to eat unless he is hungry. Will is subject to desire. But we are free; everyone feels it.

The agnostic says this idea is a delusion. Then, how prove the world? Its only proof is that we all see it and feel it; so just as much we all feel freedom. If universal consensus affirms this world, then it must be accepted as affirming freedom; but freedom is not of the will as it is. The constitutional belief of man in freedom is the basis of all reasoning. Freedom is of the will as it was before it became bound. The very idea of free-will shows every moment man's struggle against bondage. The free can be only one, the Unconditioned, the Infinite, the Unlimited. Freedom in man is now a memory, an attempt towards freedom.

Everything in the universe is struggling to complete a circle, to return to its source, to return to its only real Source, *Atman*. The search for happiness is a struggle to find the balance, to restore the equilibrium. Morality is the struggle of the bound will to get free and is the proof that we have come from perfection.

* * * *

The idea of duty is the midday sun of misery scorching the very soul. "O king, drink this one drop of nectar and be happy." ("I am not the doer," this is the nectar.)

Let there be action without reaction; action is pleasant, all misery is reaction. The child puts its hand in the flame, that is pleasure; but when its system reacts, then comes the pain of burning. When we can stop that reaction, then we have nothing to fear. Control the brain and do not let it read the record; be the witness and do not react, only thus can you be happy. The happiest moments we ever know are when we entirely forget ourselves. Work of your own free will, not from duty. We have no duty. This world is just a gymnasium in which we play; our life is an eternal holiday.

The whole secret of existence is to have no fear. Never fear what will become of you, depend on no one. Only the moment you reject all help are you free. The full sponge can absorb no more.

* * * *

Even fighting in self-defence is wrong, though it is higher than fighting in aggression. There is no "righteous" indignation, because indignation comes from not recognizing "sameness" in all things.

SUNDAY, *July 14th.*

Philosophy in India means that through which we see God, the *rationale* of religion; so no Hindu would ever ask for a link between religion and philosophy.

Concrete, generalized, abstract are the three stages in the process of philosophy. The highest abstraction in which all things agree, is the

One. In religion we have, first, symbols and forms, next mythology, and last, philosophy. The first two are for the time being; philosophy is the underlying basis of all and the others are only stepping stones in the struggle to reach the Ultimate.

In Western religion the idea is that without the New Testament and Christ there could be no religion. A similar belief exists in Judaism with regard to Moses and the Prophets, because these religions are dependent upon mythology only. Real religion, the highest, rises above mythology; it can never rest upon that. Modern science has really made the foundations of religion strong. That the whole universe is one is scientifically demonstrable. What the metaphysicians call "being" the physicist calls "matter," but there is no real fight between the two, for both are one. Though an atom is invisible, unthinkable, yet in it are the whole power and potency of the universe. That is exactly what the Vedantist says of *Atman*. All sects are really saying the same thing in different words.

Vedânta and modern science both posit a self-evolving Cause. In Itself are all the causes. Take for example the potter shaping a pot. The potter is the primal cause, the clay the material cause, and the wheel the instrumental cause; but the *Atman* is all three. *Atman* is cause and manifestation too. The Vedantist says, the universe is not real, it is only apparent. Nature is God seen through nescience. The Pantheists say, God has become nature or this world; the Advaitists affirm that God is appearing as this world, but He is not this world.

We can only know experience as a mental process, a fact in the mind as well as a mark in the brain. We cannot push the brain back or forward, but we can the mind; it can stretch over all time, past, present and future, and so facts in the mind are eternally preserved. All facts are already generalized in mind, which is omnipresent.*

Kant's great achievement was the discovery that "time, space and causation are modes of thought," but Vedânta taught this ages ago and called it "*Mâyâ*." Schopenhauer stands on reason only and rationalizes the Vedas... Sankara maintained the orthodoxy of the Vedas.

* * * *

"Treeness" or the idea tree, found out among trees, is knowledge, and the highest knowledge is One. . . . .

Personal God is the last generalization of the

---

*As the entire creation existing in Space, Time and Causation can never exist beyond mind or memory, manifesting itself as thinking, feeling and willing, therefore the whole of space, time and causation must have to be in it. Hence mind is omnipresent. Individual mind is a portion of the omnipresent or universal mind almost shut up in a body like a gulf or a bit of the ocean mostly surrounded by land leaving a narrow opening which joins it to the ocean.

universe, only hazy, not clear-cut and philosophic. . . . .

Unity is self-evolving, out of which everything comes. . . . .

Physical science is to find out facts, metaphysics is the thread to bind the flowers into a bouquet. Every abstraction is metaphysical; even putting manure at the root of a tree involves a process of abstraction. . . . .

Religion includes the concrete, the more generalized and the ultimate unity. Do not stick to particularizations. Get to the principle, to the One.

* * * *

Devils are machines of darkness, angels are machines of light; but both are machines. Man alone is alive. Break the machine, strike the balance,* and then man can become free.

---

* Find out that the relationship between yourself and the machine is as between a worker and his instrument. Never identify yourself with it.

This is the only world where man can work out his salvation.

"Whom the Self chooses" is true. Election is true, but put it within. As an external and fatalistic doctrine, it is horrible.

MONDAY, *July 15th.*

Where there is polyandry, as in Thibet, women are physically stronger than the men. When the English go there, these women carry large men up the mountains.

In Malabar, although of course polyandry does not obtain there, the women lead in everything. Exceptional cleanliness is apparent everywhere and there is the greatest impetus to learning. When I myself was in that country, I met many women who spoke good Sanskrit, while in the rest of India not one woman in a million can speak it. Mastery elevates and servitude debases. Malabar has never been conquered either by the Portuguese, or by the Mussulmans.

The Dravidians were a non-Aryan race of Central Asia, who preceded the Aryans, and those of Southern India were the most civilized. Women with them stood higher than men. They subsequently divided, some going to Egypt, others to Babylonia, and the rest remaining in India.

TUESDAY, *July 16th.* (*Sankara*)

Adrishtam, the "unseen cause," leads us to sacrifice and worship, which in turn produce seen results; so we must first hear, then think or reason, and then meditate upon *Brahman*.

The result of works and the result of knowledge are two different things. "Do" and "Do not do" are the background of all morality, but they really belong only to the body and the mind. All happiness and misery are inextricably connected with the senses, and body is necessary to experience them. The higher the body, the higher the standard of virtue, even up to Brahmâ ; but all have bodies. As long as there is a body, there must be pleasure and pain ; only when one has got rid of the body can one escape them. The *Atman* is bodiless, says Sankara.

No law can make ,you free, you *are* free. Nothing can give you freedom, if you have it not already. The *Atman* is self-illumined. Cause and effect do not reach there, and this disembodiedness is freedom. Beyond what was, or is, or is to be is *Brahman*. As an effect, freedom would have no value ; it would be a compound, and as such would contain the seeds of bondage. It is the one real factor, not to be attained, but the real nature of the soul.

Work and worship, however, are necessary to take away the veil, to lift off the bondage and illusion. They do not give us freedom, but all the same, without effort on our own part we do not open our eyes and see what we are. Sankara says further that *Advaita-Vedânta* is the crowning glory of the Vedas; but the lower Vedas are also necessary, because they teach work and worship and through these many come to the Lord. Others may come without any help but *Advaita*. Work and worship lead to the same result as *Advaita*.

Books cannot teach God, but they can destroy ignorance; their action is negative. To hold to the books and at the same time open the way to freedom, is Sankara's great achievement. But after all, it is a kind of hair-splitting. Give man first the concrete, then raise him to the highest by slow degrees. This is the effort of the various religions and explains their existence and why each is suited to some stage of development. The very books are a part of the ignorance they help to dispel. Their duty is to drive out the ignorance that has come upon knowledge. "Truth shall drive out untruth." You are free and cannot be made so. So long as you have a creed, you have no God. "He who knows he knows, knows nothing." Who can know the Knower? There are two eternal facts in existence, God and the universe. The former unchangeable, the latter changeable. The world exists eternally. Where your mind cannot grasp the amount of change, you call it eternity...You see the stone or the *bas relief* on it, but not both at once; yet both are one.

* * * *

Can you make yourself at rest even for a second? All *Yogis* say you can.

* * * *

The greatest sin is to think yourself weak. No one is greater; realize you are *Brahman*. Nothing has power except what you give it. We are beyond the sun, the stars, the universe.

Teach the Godhood of man. Deny evil, create none. Stand up and say, I am the master, the master of all. We forge the chain and we alone can break it.

No action can give you freedom; only knowledge can make you free. Knowledge is irresistible; the mind cannot take it or reject it. When it comes, the mind has to accept it; so it is not a work of the mind, only, its expression comes in the mind.

Work or worship is to bring you back to your own nature. It is an entire illusion that the Self is the body; so even while living here in the body, we can be free. The body has nothing in common with the Self. Illusion is taking the real for the unreal—not "nothing at all."

WEDNESDAY, *July 17th.*

Râmânuja divides the universe into *Chit*, *Achit* and *Isvara*; man, Nature and God; conscious, subconscious and superconscious. Sankara, on the contrary, says that *Chit*, the soul, is the same as God. God *is* truth, *is* knowledge, *is* infinity ; these are not qualities. Any thought of God is a qualification and all that can be said of him is "*Om tat sat.*"

Sankara further asks, can you see existence separate from everything else ? Where is the differentiation between two objects ? Not in sense perception, else all would be one in it. We have to perceive in sequence. In getting knowledge of what a thing is, we get also something which it is not. The *differentiae* are in the memory and are got by comparison with what is stored there. Difference is not in the nature of a thing, it is in the brain. Homogeneous one is outside, *differentiae* are inside (in the mind) ; so the idea of " many " is the creation of the mind.

Differentiae become qualities when they are separate, but joined in one object. We cannot say positively what differentiation is. All that we see and feel about things is pure and simple existence, "*isness*" All else is in us. Being is the only positive proof we have of anything. All differentiation is really "secondary reality," as the snake in the rope, because the serpent too had a certain reality, in that *something* was seen although misapprehended. When the knowledge of the rope becomes negative, the knowledge of the snake becomes positive, and *vice versa*; but the fact that you see only one does not prove that the other is non-existent. The idea of the world is an obstruction covering the idea of God, and is to be removed, but it does have an existence.

Sankara says again, perception is the last proof of existence. It is self-effulgent and self-conscious, because to go beyond the senses we should still need perception. Perception is independent of the senses, of all instruments, unconditioned. There can be no perception without consciousness; perception has self-luminosity, which in a lesser degree is called consciousness. Not one act of perception can be unconscious; in fact, consciousness is the nature of perception. Existence and perception are one thing, not two things joined together. That which needs no cause is infinite, so as perception is the last proof of itself, it is eternal. It is always subjective; perception itself is its own perceiver. Perception is not in the mind, but perception brings mind. It is absolute, the only knower, so perception is really the *Atman*. Perception itself perceives, but the *Atman* cannot be a knower, because a "knower" becomes such by the action of knowledge; but Sankara says "this *Atman* is not I" because the consciousness "I am" (*aham*) is not in the *Atman*. We are but the reflections of that *Atman*; and *Atman* and *Brahman* are one.

When you talk and think of the Absolute, you have to do it in the relative, so all these logical arguments apply. In *Yoga*, perception and realization are one. *Visishtâdvaita*, of which Râmânuja is the exponent, is seeing partial unity and is a step toward *Advaita*. *Visishtam* means differentiation. *Prakriti* is the nature of the world and change comes upon it. Changeful thoughts expressed in changeful words can never prove the Absolute. You reach only something that is minus certain qualities, not *Brahman* Itself; only a verbal unification, the highest abstraction, but not the non-existence of the relative.

THURSDAY, *July 18th.* (*The lesson to-day was mainly Sankara's argument against the conclusions of the Sânkhya philosophy.*)

The *Sânkhyas* say that consciousness is a compound, and beyond that, the last analysis gives us the *Purusha*, Witness; but that there are many *purushas*, each of us is one. *Advaita* on the contrary, affirms that *purushas* can be only One. That *Purusha* cannot be conscious, unconscious or have any qualification, for either these qualities would bind, or they would eventually cease ; so the One must be without any qualities, even knowledge, and It cannot be the cause of the universe or of anything. "In the beginning, existence only, One without a second," says the Vedas.

* * * *

The presence of *sattva* with knowledge does not prove that *sattva* is the cause of knowledge; on the contrary *sattva* calls out what was already existing in man, as the fire heats an iron ball placed near it by arousing the heat latent in it, not by entering into the ball.

Sankara says, knowledge is not a bondage, because it is the nature of God. The world ever is, whether manifested or unmanifested; so an eternal object exists.

Jnâna-bala-kriya (knowledge, power, activity) is God. Nor does He need form, because the finite only needs form to interpose as an obstruction to catch and hold infinite knowledge; but God really needs no such help. There is no "moving soul," there is only one *Atman*. *Jiva* (individual soul) is the conscious ruler of this body, in whom the five life principles come into unity, and yet that very *jiva* is the *Atman*, because all is *Atman*. What you think about it, is your delusion and not in the *jiva*. You are God and whatever else you may think is wrong. You must worship the Self in Krishna, not Krishna as Krishna, Only by worshipping the Self can freedom be won. Even personal God is but the Self objectified. "Intense search after my own reality is *Bhakti*" says Sankara.

All the means we take to reach God are true; it is only like trying to find the pole star by locating it through the stars that are around it.

* * * *

The *Bhagavad Gitâ* is the best authority on Vedânta.

FRIDAY, *July 19th.*

So long as I say "you" I have the right to speak of God protecting us. When I see another, I must take all the consequences and put in the third, the Ideal, which stands between us; that is the apex of the triangle. The vapor becomes snow, then water, then Ganges; but when it is vapor, there is no Ganges, and when it is water, we think of no vapor in it. The idea of creation or change is inseparably connected with will. So long as we perceive this world in motion, we have to conceive will behind it. Physics prove the utter delusion of the senses; nothing really is as we see, hear, feel, smell, taste it. Certain vibrations producing certain results affect our senses; we know only relative truth.

The Sanskrit word for truth is "Isness" (*sat*). From our present standpoint this world appears to us as will and consciousness. Personal God is as much an entity for Himself as we are for ourselves, and no more. God can also be seen as a form, just as we are seen. As men we must have a God; as gods we need none. This is why Sri Râmakrishna constantly saw the Divine Mother ever present with him, more real than any other thing around him; but in *Samâdhi* all went but the Self. Personal God comes nearer and nearer until He melts away and there is no more personal God and no more "I"; all is merged in Self.

Consciousness is a bondage. The argument from design claims that intelligence precedes form; but if intelligence is the cause of anything, it itself is in its turn an effect. It is *Mâyâ*. God creates us and we create God and this is *Mâyâ*. The circle is unbroken ; mind creates body and body creates mind; the egg brings the chicken, the chicken the egg ; the tree the seed, the seed the tree. The world is neither entirely differentiated nor yet entirely homogeneous. Man is free and must rise above both sides. Both are right in their place ; but to teach truth, " isness," we must transcend all that we now know of existence, will, consciousness, doing, going, knowing. There is no real individuality of the *jiva* (separate soul); eventually it, as a compound, will go to pieces. Only that which is beyond further analysis is "simple " and that alone is truth, freedom, immortality, bliss. All struggles for the preservation of this illusive individuality are really vices. All struggles to lose this individuality are virtues. Everything in the universe is trying to break down this individuality, either consciously or unconsciously. All morality is based upon the destruction of separateness or false individuality, because that is the cause of all sin. Morality exists first, later religion codifies it. Customs come first and then mythology follows to explain them. While things are happening, they cóme by a higher law than reasoning ; that arises later in the attempt to understand them. Reasoning is not the motive power, it is "chewing the cud" afterwards. Reason is the historian of the actions of the human being.

* * * *

Buddha was a great Vedantist (for Buddhism was really only an offshoot of Vedânta), and Sankara is often called a "hidden Buddhist." Buddha made the analysis, Sankara made the synthesis out of it. Buddha never bowed down to anything, neither Veda, nor caste, nor priest, nor custom. He fearlessly reasoned so far as reason could take him. Such a fearless search for truth and such love for every living thing the world has never seen. Buddha was the Washington of the religious world; he conquered a throne only to give it to the world, as Washington did to the American people. He sought nothing for himself.

SATURDAY, *July 20th.*

Perception is our only real knowledge or religion. Talking about it for ages will never make us know our soul. There is no difference between theories and atheism. In fact, the atheist is the truer man. Every step I take in the light is mine forever. When you go to a country and see it, then it is yours. We have each to see for ourselves; teachers can only "bring the food," we must eat it to be nourished. Argument can never prove God save as a logical conclusion.

It is impossible to find God outside of ourselves. Our own souls contribute all the divinity that is outside of us. We are the greatest temple. The objectification is only a faint imitation of what we see within ourselves.

Concentration of the powers of the mind is our only instrument to help us see God. If you know one soul (your own), you know all souls, past, present and to come. The will concentrates the mind, certain things excite and control this will, such as reason, love, devotion breathing, etc. The concentrated mind is a lamp that shows us every corner of the soul.

No one method can suit all. These different methods are not steps necessary to be taken one after another. Ceremonials are the lowest form next God external and after that God internal. In some cases gradation may be needed, but in many only one way is required It would be the height of folly to say to everyone, "you must pass through *Karma* and *Bhakti* before you can reach *Jnânam.*"

Stick to your reason until you reach something higher, and you will know it to be higher because it will not jar with reason. The stage beyond consciousness is inspiration (*Samâdhi*) but never mistake hysterical trances for the real thing. It is a terrible thing to claim this inspiration falsely, to mistake instinct for inspiration. There is no external test for inspiration, we know it ourselves ; our guardian against mistake is negative,—the voice of reason. All religion is going beyond reason, but the reason is the only guide to get there. Instinct is like ice, reason is the water, and inspiration is the subtlest form or vapor ; one follows the other. Everywhere is this eternal sequence, unconsciousness, consciousness, intelligence ; matter, body, mind ; and to us it seems as if the chain began with the particular link we first lay hold of. Arguments on both sides are of equal weight and both are true. We must reach beyond both, to where there is neither the one nor the other. These successions are all *Mâyâ*.

Religion is above reason, supernatural. Faith is not belief, it is the grasp on the Ultimate, an illumination. First hear, then reason and find out all that reason can give about the *Atman*; let the flood of reason flow over it, then take what remains. If nothing remains, thank God you have escaped a superstition. When you have determined that nothing *can* take away the *Atman*, that it stands every test, hold fast to this and teach it to all. Truth cannot be partial; it is for the good of all. Finally, in perfect rest and peace meditate upon it, concentrate your mind upon it, make yourself one with it. Then no speech is needed; silence will carry the truth. Do not spend your energy in talking, but meditate in silence ; and do not let the rush of the outside world disturb you. When your mind is in the highest state, you are unconscious of it. Accumulate power in silence and become a dynamo of spirituality. What can a beggar give ? Only a king can give, and he only when he wants nothing himself.

* * * *

Hold your money merely as custodian for what is God's. Have no attachment for it. Let name and fame and money go ; they are a terrible bondage. Feel the wonderful atmosphere of freedom. You are free, free, free ! Oh blessed am I ! Freedom am I ! I am the Infinite ! In my soul I can find no beginning and no end. All is my Self. Say this unceasingly.

SUNDAY, *July* 21*st*. (*Patanjali's Yoga Aphorisms.*)

Yoga is the science of restraining the *chitta*

(mind) from breaking into *vritti* (modifications.) Mind is a mixture of sensation and feelings, or action and reaction, so it cannot be permanent. The mind has a fine body and through this it works on the gross body. Vedânta says that behind the mind is the real Self. It accepts the other two, but posits a third, the Eternal, the Ultimate, the last analysis, the unit, where there is no further compound. Birth is *re*-composition, death is *de*-composition, and the final analysis is where *Atman* is found; there being no further division possible, the perduring is reached.

The whole ocean is present at the back of each wave and all manifestations are waves, some very big, some small; yet all are the ocean in their essence, the whole ocean, but as waves each is a part. When the waves are stilled, then all is one; "a spectator without a spectacle" says Patanjali. When the mind is active, the *Atman* is mixed up with it. The repetition of old forms in quick succession is memory.

Be unattached. Knowledge is power, and getting one you get the other. By knowledge you can even banish the material world. When you can mentally get rid of one quality after another from any object until all are gone, you can at will make the object itself disappear from your consciousness.

Those who are ready, advance very quickly and can become *Yogis* in six months. The less developed may take several years; and anyone by faithful work and by giving up everything else and devoting himself solely to practice can reach the goal in twelve years. *Bhakti* will bring you there without any of these mental gymnastics, but it is a slower way. *

* Here by Bhakti Swâmiji does not mean intense or undivided love for God. He has already taught " Extreme Love and Highest knowledge are one" and again in defining it he says. "This absolute and continuous remembrance of the Lord is what is meant by Bhakti"; so by

Isvara is the *Atman* as seen or grasped by mind. His highest name is *Om*, so repeat it, meditate on it and think of all its wonderful nature and attributes. Repeating the *Om* continually is the only true worship. It is not a word, it is God Himself.

Religion gives you nothing new; it only takes off obstacles and lets you see your Self. Sickness is the first great obstacle; a healthy body is the best instrument. Melancholy is an almost insuperable barrier. If you have once known *Brahman*, never after can you be melancholy. Doubt, want of perseverance, mistaken ideas, are other obstacles.

* * * *

Prânas are subtle energies, sources of motion. There are ten in all, five inward and five out-

---

Bhakti he means here, Love which is not yet whole-souled. There are few Bhaktas who love God for God's sake. Most of them love Him for His omnipotence, wherewith he can fulfil their desires for things other than Himself.

ward. One great current flows upwards, and the other downwards. *Prânayâma* is controlling the *prânas* through breathing. Breath is the fuel, *prâna* is the steam and the body is the engine. *Prânayâma* has three parts, *puraka* (in-breathing), *kumbhaka* (holding the breath) *rechaka* (out-breathing).

* * * *

The *Guru* is the conveyance in which the spiritual influence is brought to you. Anyone can teach, but the spirit must be passed on by the *Guru* to the *Sishya* (disciple) and that will fructify. The relation between *sishyas* is that of brotherhood, and this is actually accepted by law in India. The *Guru* passes the thought power, the *mantram,* that he has received from those before him; and nothing can be done without a *Guru.* In fact, great danger ensues. Usually without a *Guru* these *yoga* practices lead to lust; but with one this seldom happens.

Each *Ishtam* has a *mantram*. The *Ishtam* is the ideal peculiar to the particular worshipper ; the *mantram* is the external word to express it. Constant repetition of the word helps to fix the ideal firmly in the mind. This method of worship prevails among religious devotees all over India.

TUESDAY, *July 23rd. (Bhagavad Gitâ. Karma Yoga).*

To attain liberation through work join yourself to work but without desire, looking for no result. Such work leads to knowledge, which in turn brings emancipation. To give up work before you *know*, leads to misery. Work done for the Self gives no bondage. Neither desire pleasure nor fear pain from work. It is the mind and body that work, not I. Tell yourself this unceasingly and realize it. Try not to know that you work.

Do all as a sacrifice or offering to the Lord.

Be in the world, but not of it, like the lotus leaf, whose roots are in the mud but which remains always pure. Let your love go to all, whatever they do to you. A blind man cannot see color, so how can we see evil except it is in us? We compare what we see outside with what we find in ourselves and pronounce judgment accordingly. If we are pure, we cannot see impurity. It may exist, but not for us. See only God in every man, woman and child; see it by the "*antarjyotis,*" "inner light," and seeing that, we can see naught else. Do not want this world, because what you desire you get. Seek the Lord and the Lord only. The more power there is, the more bondage, the more fear. How much more afraid and miserable are we than the ant! Get out of it all and come to the Lord. Seek the science of the maker and not that of the made.

"I am the doer and the deed." "He who can

stem the tide of lust and anger is a great *Yogi.*"

"Only by practice and non-attachment can we conquer mind."

* * * *

Our Hindu ancestors sat down and thought on God and morality, and so have we brains to use for the same ends; but in the rush of trying to get gain, we are likely to lose them again.

* * * *

The body has in itself a certain power of curing itself and many things can rouse this curative power into action, such as mental conditions or medicine, or exercise, etc. As long as we are disturbed by physical conditions, so long we need the help of physical agencies. Not until we have got rid of bondage to the nerves, can we disregard them.

There is unconscious mind, but it is below consciousness, which is just one part of the human organism. Philosophy is guess work about the mind. Religion is based upon sense contact, upon seeing, the only basis of knowledge. What comes in contact with the superconscious mind is fact. "*Aptas*" are those who have "sensed" religion. The proof is that if you follow their method, you too will see. Each science requires its own particular method and instruments. An astronomer cannot show you the rings of Saturn by the aid of all the pots and pans in the kitchen. He needs a telescope. So, to see the great facts of religion, the method of those who have already seen must be followed. The greater the science, the more varied the means of studying it. Before we came into the world God provided the means to get out; so all we have to do is to find the means. But do not fight over methods. Look only for realization and choose the best method you can find to suit you. Eat the mangoes and let the rest quarrel over the basket. *See* Christ, then you will be a Christian. All else is talk ; the less talking the better.

The message makes the messenger. The Lord makes the temple ; not *vice versa.*

Learn until "the glory of the Lord shines through your face," as it shone through the face of Svetaketu.

Guess against guess makes fight ; but talk of what you have seen and no human heart can resist it. Paul was converted against his will by realization.

TUESDAY AFTERNOON. (*After dinner there was a short conversation in the course of which the Swâmi said* :)

Delusion creates delusion. Delusion creates itself and destroys itself, such is *Mâyâ.* All knowledge (so-called) being based on *Mâyâ,* is a vicious circle and in time that very knowledge destroys itself. "Let go the rope," delusion cannot touch the *Atman*. When we lay hold of the rope,—identify ourselves with *Mâyâ*, she has power over us. Let go of it, be the Witness only, then you can admire the picture of the universe undisturbed.

WEDNESDAY, *July 24th.*

The powers acquired by the practice of *Yoga* are not obstacles for the *Yogi* who is perfect, but are apt to be so for the beginner, through the wonder and pleasure excited by their exercise. *Siddhis* are the powers which mark success in the practice and they may be produced by various means, such as the repetition of a *mantram*, by *yoga* practice, meditation, fasting, or even by the use of herbs and drugs. The *Yogi* who has conquered all interest in the powers acquired and who renounces all virtue arising from his actions, comes into the " cloud of virtue" (name of one of the states of *Samâ-*

dhi) and radiates holiness as a cloud rains water.

Meditation is on a series of objects, concentration is on one object.

Mind is cognized by the *Atman*, but it is not self-illuminated. The *Atman* cannot be the cause of anything. How can it be? How can the *Purusha* join itself to *Prakriti* (Nature) ? It does not; it is only illusively thought to do so.

* * * *

Learn to help without pitying, or feeling that there is any misery. Learn to be the same to enemy and to friend, then when you can do that and no longer have any desires, the goal is attained.

Cut down the banyan tree of desire with the axe of non-attachment and it will vanish utterly. It is all illusion. "He from whom blight and delusion have fallen, he who has conquered the evils of association, he alone is *âzâd* (free)."

To love anyone personally is bondage. Love all alike, then all desires fall off.

Time, the "eater of everything," comes and all has to go. Why try to improve the earth, to paint the butterfly? It all has to go at last. Do not be mere white mice in a treadmill, working always aud never accomplishing anything. Every desire is fraught with evil, whether the desire itself be good or evil. It is like a dog jumping for a piece of meat which is ever receding from his reach, and dying a dog's death at last. Do not be like that. Cut off all desire.

* * * *

Paramâtman as ruling *Mâyâ* is *Isvara*; *Paramâtman* as under *Mâyâ* is *Jivâtman*. *Mâyâ* is the sum-total of manifestation and will utterly vanish.

Tree-nature is *Mâyâ*, it is really God-nature which we see under the veil of *Mâyâ*. The "why" of anything is in *Mâyâ*. To ask why *Mâyâ* came is a useless question, because the answer can never be given in *Mâyâ*, and beyond *Mâyâ* who will ask it? Evil creates "why" not "why" the evil, and it is evil that asks "why"? Illusion destroys illusion. Reason itself, being based upon contradiction, is a circle and has to kill itself. Sense perception is an inference and yet all inference comes from perception.

Ignorance reflecting the light of God is seen; but by itself it is zero. The cloud would not appear except as the sunlight falls on it.

There were four travellers who came to a high wall. The first one climbed with difficulty to the top and without looking back, jumped over. The second clambered up the wall, looked over and with a shout of delight disappeared. The third in his turn climbed to the top, looked where his companions had gone, laughed with joy and followed them. But the fourth one came back to tell what had happened to his fellow-travellers. The sign to us that there is something beyond is the laugh that rings back from those great ones who have plunged from *Mâyâ's* wall.

*   *   *   *

Separating ourselves from the Absolute and attributing certain qualities to it gives us *Isvara.* It is the Reality of the universe as seen through our mind. Personal devil is the misery of the world seen through the minds of the superstitious.

THURSDAY, *July 25th.* (*Patanjali's Yoga Aphorisms.*)

"Things may be done, caused to be done, or approved of," and the effect upon us is nearly equal.

Complete continence gives great intellectual and spiritual power. The *Brahmacharin* must be sexually pure in thought, word and deed. Lose regard for the body; get rid of the consciousness of it so far as possible.

Asana (posture) must be steady and pleasant, and constant practice, identifying the mind with the Infinite, will bring this about.

Continual attention to one object is contemplation.

When a stone is thrown into still water, many circles are made, each distinct but all interacting; so with our minds; only in us the action is unconscious, while with the *Yogi* it is conscious. We are spiders in a web and *yoga* practice will enable us like the spider to pass along any strand of the web we please. Non-*Yogis* are bound to the particular spot where they are.

* * * *

To injure another creates bondage and hides the truth. Negative virtues are not enough; we have to conquer *Mâyâ* and then she will follow us. We only deserve things when they have ceased to bind us. When the bondage ceases, really and truly, all things come to us. Only those who want nothing are masters of Nature.

Take refuge in some soul who has already broken his bondage, and in time he will free you through his mercy. Higher still, is to take refuge in the Lord (*Isvara*), but it is the most difficult; only once in a century can one be found who has really done it. Feel nothing, know nothing, do nothing, have nothing, give up all to God and say utterly, "Thy will be done." We only dream this bondage. Wake up and let it go. Take refuge in God, only so can we cross the desert of *Mâyâ*. "Let go thy hold, *Sanyâsin* bold, say '*Om tat sat, Om*!'".

It is our privilege to be allowed to be charitable, for only so can we grow. The poor man suffers that we may be helped; let the giver kneel down and give thanks, let the receiver stand up and permit. See the Lord back of every being and give to Him. When we cease to see evil, the world must end for us, since to rid us of that mistake is its only object. To think there is any imperfection creates it. Thoughts of strength and perfection alone can cure it. Do what good you can, some evil will inhere in it; but do all without regard to personal result, give up all results to the Lord, then neither good nor evil will affect you.

Doing work is not religion, but work done rightly leads to freedom. In reality all pity is darkness, because whom to pity? Can you pity God? And is there anything else? Thank God for giving you this world as a moral gymnasium to help your development, but never imagine you can help the world. Be grateful to him who curses you, for he gives you a mirror to show what cursing is, also a chance to practise self-restraint ; so bless him and be glad. Without exercise power cannot come out, without the mirror we cannot see ourselves.

Unchaste imagination is as bad as unchaste action. Controlled desire leads to the highest result. Transform the sexual energy into spiritual energy, but do not emasculate, because that is throwing away the power. The stronger this force, the more can be done with it. Only a powerful current of water can do hydraulic mining.

What we need to-day is to know that there is a God and that we can see and feel Him here and now. A Chicago professor says, "Take care of this world, God will take care of the next." What nonsense ! If we can take care of this world, what need of a gratuitous Lord to take care of the other !

FRIDAY, *July 26th.* (*Brihadâranyakopanishad.*)

Love all things only through and for the Self. *Yajnavalkya* said to *Maitreyi,* his wife, "Through the *Atman* we know all things." The *Atman* can never be the object of knowledge, nor can the Knower be known. He who knows he is the *Atman,* he is a law unto himself. He knows he is the universe and its creator.

* * * *

Perpetuating old myths in the form of allegories and giving them undue importance fosters superstition and is really weakness. Truth must have no compromise. Teach truth and make no apology for any superstition ; neither drag truth down to the level of the listener.

SATURDAY, *July 27th.* (*Kathopanishad.*)

Learn not the truth of the Self save from one who has realized it; in all others it is mere talk. Realization is beyond virtue and vice., beyond future and past; beyond all the pairs of opposites. "The stainless one sees the Self and an eternal calm comes in the soul." Talking, arguing and reading books, the highest flights of the intellect, the Vedas themselves, all these cannot give knowledge of the Self.

In us are the two,—the God-soul and the man-soul. The sages know that the latter is but the shadow, that the former is the only real Sun.

Unless we join the mind with the senses, we get no report from eyes, nose, ears, etc. The external organs are used by the power of the mind. Do not let the senses go outside and then you can get rid of body and the external world.

This very "x" which we see here as an

external world, the departed see as heaven or hell according to their own mental states. Here and hereafter are two dreams, the latter modelled on the former; get rid of both, all is omnipresent, all is now. Nature, body and mind go to death, not we; we never go nor come. The man Swâmi Vivekânanda is in Nature, is born and dies; but the Self which we see as Swâmi Vivekânanda is never born and never dies. It is the eternal and unchangeable Reality.

The power of the mind is the same, whether we divide it into five senses or whether we see only one. A blind man says, "Every thing has a distinct echo, so I clap my hands and get that echo and then I can tell everything that is around me." So in a fog the blind man could safely lead the seeing man. Fog or darkness makes no difference to him.

Control the mind, cut off the senses, then you are a *Yogi;* after that all the rest will come.

Refuse to hear, to see, to smell, to taste; take away the mental power from the external organs. You continually do it unconsciously, as when your mind is absorbed; so you can learn to do it consciously. The mind can put the senses where it pleases. Get rid of the fundamental superstition that we are obliged to act through the body. We are not. Go into your own room and get the Upanishads out of your own Self. You are the greatest book that ever was or ever will be, the infinite depositary of all that is. Until the inner teacher opens, all outside teaching is in vain. It must lead to the opening of the book of the heart to have any value.

The will is the "still small voice," the real Ruler who says "do" and "do not." It has done all that binds us. The ignorant will leads to bondage, the knowing will can free us. The will can be made strong in thousands of ways;

every way is a kind of *Yoga*, but the systematized *Yoga* accomplishes the work more quickly. *Bhakti, Karma, Râja* and *Jnâna Yoga* get over the ground more effectively. Put on all powers, philosophy, work, prayer, meditation ; crowd all sail, put on all head of steam, and reach the goal. The sooner, the better.

* * * * *

Baptism is external purification symbolizing the internal. It is of Buddhist origin.

The Eucharist is a survival of a very ancient custom of savage tribes. They sometimes killed their great chiefs and ate their flesh in order to obtain in themselves the qualities that made their leaders great. They believed that in such a way, the characteristics that made the chief brave and wise would become theirs and make the whole tribe brave and wise, instead of only one man. Human sacrifice was also a Jewish idea and one that clung to them despite many chastisements from Jehovah. Jesus was gentle and loving, but to fit him into Jewish beliefs, the idea of human sacrifice in the form of atonement or as a human scape-goat, had to come in. This cruel idea made Christianity depart from the teachings of Jesus himself and develop a spirit of persecution and bloodshed.

*   *   *   *   *

Say "it is my nature," never say "it is my duty" to do anything whatever.

"Truth alone triumphs, not untruth." Stand upon Truth and you have got God.

*   *   *   *

From the earliest times in India the Brahmin caste have held themselves beyond all law; they claim to be gods. They are poor, but their weakness is that they seek power. Here are about sixty millions of people who are good and moral and hold no property, and they are what they are because from their birth they are taught that they are above law, above punishment. They feel themselves to be "twice-born," to be sons of God.

SUNDAY, *July 28th* (*Avadhuta Gitâ or "Song of the Purified" by Dattâtreya.**)

"All knowledge depends upon calmness of mind."

"He who has filled the universe, He who is Self in self, How shall I salute Him !"

To know the *Atman* as my nature is both knowledge and realization. "I am He, there is not the least doubt of it."

"No thought, no word, no deed, creates a bondage for me. I am beyond the senses, I am knowledge and Bliss."

There is neither existence nor non-existence, all is *Atman*. Shake off all ideas of relativity ;

* Dattatreya was a sage, the son of Atri and Anasuya, and was an incarnation of Brahmâ, Vishnu and Maheswara.

shake off all superstitions; let caste and birth and *devas* and all else vanish. Why talk of being and becoming ? Give up talking of Dualism and Advaitism ! When were you two, that you talk of two or one ? The universe is this Holy One and He alone. Talk not of *Yoga* to make you pure ; you are pure by your very nature. None can teach you.

Men like him who wrote this song are what keep religion alive. They have actually realized ; they care for nothing, feel nothing done to the body, care not for heat and cold or danger or anything. They sit still and enjoy the bliss of *Atman*, while red hot coals burn their body, and they feel them not.

"When the threefold bondage of knower, knowledge and known ceases, there is the *Atman*."

"Where the delusion of bondage and freedom ceases, there the *Atman* is."

"What if you have controlled the mind, what if you have not? What if you have money, what if you have not? You are the *Atman*, ever pure. Say, 'I am the *Atman*. No bondage ever came near me. I am the changeless sky; clouds of belief may pass over me, but they do not touch me'."

"Burn virtue, burn vice. Freedom is baby talk. I am that immortal Knowledge. I am that purity."

"No one was ever bound, none was ever free. There is none but me. I am the Infinite, the Ever-Free. Talk not to me! What can change me, the essence of knowledge! Who can teach, who can be taught?"

Throw argument, throw philosophy into the ditch.

"Only a slave sees slaves, the deluded delusion, the impure impurity."

Place, time, causation are all delusions. It

is your disease that you think you are bound and will be free. You are the Unchangeable. Talk not. Sit down and let all things melt away, they are but dreams. There is no differentiation, no distinction, it is all superstition ; therefore be silent and know what you are.

"I am the essence of bliss." Follow no ideal, you are all there is. Fear naught, you are the essence of existence. Be at peace. Do not disturb yourself. You never were in bondage, you never were virtuous or sinful. Get rid of all these delusions and be at peace. Whom to worship ? Who worships ? All is the *Atman*. To speak, to think is superstition. Repeat over and over, "I am *Atman*," "I am *Atman*." Let everything else go.

MONDAY, *July 29th*.

We sometimes indicate a thing by describing

its surroundings. When we say "*Satchidânanda*" ("Existence—Knowledge—Bliss"), we are merely indicating the shores of an indescribable Beyond. Not even can we say "is" about it, for that too is relative. Any imagination, any concept is in vain ; *neti*, *neti* ("not this, not this") is all that can be said, for even to think is to limit and so to lose.

The senses cheat you day and night. Vedânta found that out ages ago ; modern science is just discovering the same fact. A picture has only length and breadth, and the painter copies Nature in her cheating by artificially giving the appearance of depth. No two people see the same world. The highest knowledge will show you that there is no motion, no change in anything ; that the very idea of it is all *Mâyâ*. Study Nature as a whole, that is, study motion. Mind and body are not our real Self ; both belong to nature, but eventually we can know the *ding an sich.* Then mind and body being transcended, all that they conceive goes. When you cease utterly to know and see the world, then you realize *Atman.* The superseding of relative knowledge is what we want. There is no infinite mind or infinite knowledge, because both mind and knowledge are limited. We are now seeing through a veil, then we reach the "x," which is the Reality of all our knowing.

If we look at a picture through a pin hole in a card board, we get an utterly mistaken notion ; yet what we see is really the picture. As we enlarge the hole, we get a clearer and clearer idea. Out of the reality we manufacture the different views in conformity with our mistaken perceptions of name and form. When we throw away the cardboard, we see the same picture, but we see it as it is. We put in all the attributes, all the errors, the picture itself is unaltered thereby. That is because *Atman* is the reality of all ; all we see is *Atman*, but not as we see it, as name and form ; they are all in our veil, in *Mâyâ*.

They are like spots in the object glass of a telescope, yet it is the light of the sun that shows us the spots ; we could not even see the illusion save for the background of reality which is *Brahman*. Swâmi Vivekânanda is just the speck on the object glass ; I am *Atman*, real, unchangeable, and that reality alone enables me to see Swâmi Vivekânanda. *Atman* is the essence of every hallucination; but the sun is never identified with the spots on the glass, it only shows them to us. Our actions, as they are evil or good, increase or decrease the "spots," but they never affect the God within us. Perfectly cleanse the mind of spots and instantly we see "I and my father are one"

We first perceive, then reason later. We

must have this perception as a fact, and it is called religion, realization. No matter if one never heard of creed or prophet or book, let him get this realization and he needs no more. Cleanse the mind, this is all of religion; and until we ourselves clear off the spots, we cannot see the Reality as it is. The baby sees no sin; he has not yet the measure of it in himself. Get rid of the defects within yourself and you will not be able to see any without. A baby sees robbery done and it means nothing to him. Once you find the hidden object in a puzzle picture, you see it ever more; so when once you are free and stainless, you see only freedom and purity in the world around. "That moment all the knots of the heart are cut asunder, all crooked places are made straight and this world vanishes as a dream." And when we awake, we wonder how we ever came to dream such trash!

"Getting Whom, misery mountain high has no power to move the soul."

With the axe of knowledge cut the wheels asunder and the *Atman* stands free, even though the old momentum carries on the wheel of mind and body. The wheel can now only go straight, can only do good. If that body does anything bad, know that the man is not "*jivan-mukta*"; he lies if he makes that claim. But it is only when the wheels have got a good straight motion (from cleansing the mind) that the axe can be applied. All purifying action deals conscious or unconscious blows on delusion. To call another a sinner is the worst thing you can do. Good action done ignorantly produces the same result and helps to break the bondage.

To identify the sun with the spots on the object glass is the fundamental error. Know the sun, the "I," to be ever unaffected by anything, and devote yourself to cleansing the spots. Man is the greatest being that ever can be. The highest worship there is, is to worship man, as Krishna, Buddha, Christ. What you want, you create. Get rid of desire.

* * * *

The angels and the departed are all here, seeing this world as heaven. The same "x" is seen by all according to their mental attitude. The best vision to be had of the "x" is here on this earth. Never want to go to heaven, that is the worst delusion. Even here, too much wealth and grinding poverty are both bondages and hold us back from religion. Three great gifts we have,—first a human body. (The human mind is the nearest reflection of God, we are "His own image.") Second, the desire to be free. Third, the help of a noble soul, who has crossed the ocean of delusion, as a teacher. When you have these three, bless the Lord; you are sure to be free.

What you only grasp intellectually may be overthrown by a new argument, but what you realize is yours forever. Talking, talking religion is but little good. Put God behind everything, man, animal, food, work, make this a habit.

Ingersoll once said to me: "I believe in making the most out of this world, in squeezing the orange dry, because this world is all we are sure of." I replied: "I know a better way to squeeze the orange of this world than you do and I get more out of it. I *know* I cannot die, so I am not in a hurry; I know there is no fear, so I enjoy the squeezing. I have no duty, no bondage of wife and children and property; I can love all men and women. Every one is God to me. Think of the joy of loving man as God! Squeeze your orange this way and get ten thousand fold more out of it. Get every single drop."

That which seems to be the will is the Atman behind, it is really free.

MONDAY AFTERNOON.

Jesus was imperfect because he did not live up fully to his own ideal, and above all because he did not give woman a place equal to man. Women did everything for him and yet he was so bound by the Jewish custom that not one was made an apostle. Still he was the greatest character next to Buddha, who in his turn was not fully perfect. Buddha, however, recognized woman's right to an equal place in religion and his first and one of his greatest disciples was his own wife, who became the head of the whole Buddhistic movement among the women of India. But we ought not to criticise these great ones, we should only look upon them as far above ourselves. Nonetheless we must not pin our faith to any man, however great; we too must become Buddhas and Christs.

No man should be judged by his defects. The great virtues a man has are his, especially his errors are the common weaknesses of humanity and should never be counted in estimating his character.

* * * *

Vira, the Sanskrit word for "heroic", is the origin of our word "virtue", because in ancient times the best fighter was regarded as the most virtuous man.

TUESDAY, *July 30th.*

Christs and Buddhas are simply occasions upon which to objectify our own inner powers. We really answer our own prayers.

It is blasphemy to think that if Jesus had never been born, humanity would not have been saved. It is horrible to thus forget the divinity in human nature, a divinity that must come out. Never forget the glory of human nature. We are the greatest God that ever was or ever will be. Christs and Buddhas are but waves on the boundless ocean which *I am.* Bow down to nothing but your own higher Self. Until you know that you are that very God of gods, there will never be any freedom for you.

All our past actions are really good because they lead us to what we ultimately become. Of whom to beg ? I am the real existence and all else is a dream save as it is I. I am the whole ocean ; do not call the little wave you have made " I " ; know it for nothing but a wave. *Satyakâma* (lover of truth) heard the inner voice telling him, " You are the infinite, the universal is in you. Control yourself and listen to the voice of your true Self."

The great prophets who do the fighting have to be less perfect than those who live silent lives of holiness, thinking great thoughts and so helping the world. These men, passing out one after another, produce as final outcome the man of power who preaches.

* * * *

Knowledge exists, man only discovers it. The Vedas are this eternal knowledge, through which God created the world. They talk high philosophy (the highest), and make this tremendous claim.

* * * *

Tell the truth boldly, whether it hurts or not. Never pander to weakness. If truth is too much for intelligent people and sweeps them away, let them go ; the sooner the better. Childish ideas are for babies and savages ; and these are not all in the nursery and the forests, some of them have fallen into the pulpits.

It is bad to stay in the church after you are grown up spiritually. Come out and die in the open air of freedom.

All progression is in the relative world. The human form is the highest and man the greatest being, because here and now we can get rid of the relative world entirely, can actually attain freedom, and this is the goal. Not only we can, but some have reached perfection ; so no matter what finer bodies come, they could only be on the relative plane and could do no more than we, for to attain freedom is all that can be done.

The angels never do wicked deeds, so they never get punished and never get saved. Blows are what awaken us and help to break the dream. They show us the insufficiency of this world and make us long to escape, to have freedom.

* * * *

A thing dimly perceived we call by one name; the same thing when fully perceived we call by another. The higher the moral nature, the higher the perception and the stronger the will.

TUESDAY AFTERNOON.

The reason of the harmony between thought and matter is because they are two sides of one thing, call it "x," which divides itself into the internal and the external.

The English word "paradise" comes from the Sanskrit *para-desa,* which was taken over into the Persian language and means literally "beyond the land" or really "the land beyond," or the other world. The old Aryans always believed in a soul, never that man was the body. Their heavens and hells were all temporary, because no effect can outlast its cause and no cause is eternal; therefore all effects must come to an end.

The whole of the Vedânta Philosophy is in this story : Two birds of golden plumage sat on the same tree. The one above, serene, majestic, immersed in his own glory ; the one below restless and eating the fruits of the tree, now sweet, now bitter. Once he ate an exceptionally bitter fruit, then he paused and looked up at the majestic bird above ; but he soon forgot about the other bird and went on eating the fruits of the tree as before. Again he ate a bitter fruit and this time he hopped up a few boughs nearer to the bird at the top. This happened many times until at last the lower bird came to the place of the upper bird and lost himself. He found all at once that there had never been two birds, but that he all the time was that upper bird, serene, majestic and immersed in his own glory.

WEDNESDAY, *July* 31*st.*

Luther drove a nail into religion when he

took away renunciation and gave us morality instead. Atheists and materialists can have ethics, but only believers in the Lord can have religion.

The wicked pay the price of the great soul's holiness. Think of that when you see a wicked man. Just as the poor man's labor pays for the rich man's luxury, so is it in the spiritual world. The terrible degradation of the masses in India is the price Nature pays for the production of great souls like Mira-bâi, Buddha, etc.*

* * * *

"I am the holiness of the holy." (Gitâ) "I am the root, each uses it in his own way, but all is I." "I do everything, you are but the occasion."

---

* For when people become very much degraded then only great souls like Mira-bâi, Buddha etc are born. (*Vide* Gitâ.)

Do not talk much, but feel the spirit within you, then you are a *Jnâni*. This is knowledge, all else is ignorance. All that is to be known is *Brahman*. It is the all.

* * * *

Sattva binds through the search for happiness and knowledge, *rajas* binds through desire, *tamas* binds through wrong perception and laziness. Conquer the two lower by *sattva*, and then give up all to the Lord and be free.

The *Bhakti Yogi* realizes *Brahman* very soon and goes beyond the three qualities.*

The will, the consciousness, the senses, desire, the passions, all these combined make what we call the "soul."

There is first the apparent self (body); second the mental self, who mistakes the body for himself (the Absolute bound by *Mâyâ*); third

* Gitâ, Chapter XII.

the *Atman*, the ever pure, the ever free. Seen partially, It is nature ; seen wholly, all Nature goes, even the memory of it is lost. There is the changeable (mortal), the eternally changeable (Nature), and the Unchangeable (Atman).

* * * *

Be perfectly hopeless, that is the highest state. What is there to hope for ? Burst asunder the bonds of hope, stand on your Self, be at rest, never mind what you do, give up all to God, but have no hypocrisy about it.

Svastha, the Sanskrit word for " standing on your own Self, " is used colloquially in India to enquire " Are you well, are you happy ? " And when Hindus would express " I saw a thing, " they say, " I saw a word-meaning " (*Padârtha*). Even this universe is a " word-meaning."

* * * *

A perfect man's body mechanically does right ; it can do only good because it is fully purified. The past momentum that carries on the wheel of body is all good. All evil tendencies are burnt out.

* * * *

" That day is indeed a bad day when we do not speak of the Lord, not a stormy day."

Only love for the Supreme Lord is true *Bhakti*. Love for any other being, however great, is not *Bhakti*. The " Supreme Lord " here means *Isvara*, the concept of which transcends what you in the West mean by the personal God. " He from whom this universe proceeds, in whom it rests, and to whom it returns, He is *Isvara*, the Eternal, the Pure, the All-Merciful, the Almighty, the Ever-Free, the All Knowing, the Teacher of all teachers, the Lord who of His own nature is inexpressible Love."

Man does not manufacture God out of his

own brain; but he can only see God in the light of his own capacity, and he attributes to Him the best of all he knows. Each attribute is the whole of God, and this signifying the whole by one quality is the metaphysical explanation of the personal God. *Isvara* is without form yet has all forms, is without qualities yet has all qualities. As human beings we have to see the trinity of existence,—God, man, Nature; and we cannot do otherwise.

But to the *Bhakta* all these philosophical distinctions are mere idle talk.. He cares nothing for argument, he does not reason, he "senses," he perceives. He wants to lose himself in pure love of God, and there have been *Bhaktas* who maintain that this is more to be desired than liberation; who say "I do not want to *be* sugar. I want to taste sugar." "I want to love and enjoy the Beloved,"

In *Bhakti-Yoga* the first essential is to want

God honestly and intensely. We want everything but God, because our ordinary desires are fulfilled by the external world. So long as our needs are confined within the limits of the physical universe, we do not feel any need for God; it is only when we have had hard blows in our lives and are disappointed with everything here that we feel the need for something higher; then we seek God.

Bhakti is not destructive; it teaches that all our faculties may become means to reach salvation. We must turn them all towards God and give to Him that love which is usually wasted on the fleeting objects of sense.

Bhakti differs from your Western idea of religion in that *Bhakti* admits no element of fear, no Being to be appeased or propitiated. There are even *Bhaktas* who worship God as their own child, so that there may remain no feeling even of awe or reverence. There can be no fear in true love, and so long as there is the least fear, *Bhakti* cannot even begin. In *Bhakti* there is also no place for begging or bargaining with God. The idea of asking God for anything is sacrilege to a *Bhakta*. He will not pray for health or wealth or even to go to heaven.

One who wants to love God, to be a *Bhakta*, must make a bundle of all these desires and leave them outside the door and then enter. He who wants to enter the realms of light must make a bundle of all "shop-keeping" religion and cast it away before he can pass the gates. It is not that you do not get what you pray for; you get everything, but it is low, vulgar, a beggar's religion. "Fool indeed is he, who living on the banks of the Ganges, digs a little well for water. Fool indeed is the man who, coming to a mine of diamonds, begins to search for glass beads." These prayers for health and wealth and material prosperity are not *Bhakti.* They are the lowest form of *Karma.* *Bhakti* is a higher thing. We are striving to come into the presence of the King of kings. We cannot get there in a beggar's dress. If we wanted to enter the presence of an emperor would we be admitted in beggar's rags? Certainly not. The lackey would drive us out of the gates. This is the Emperor of emperors and never can we come before Him in beggar's garb. Shop-keepers never have admission there, buying and selling will not do there at all. You read in the Bible that Jesus drove the buyers and sellers out of the temple.

So it goes without saying that the first task in becoming a *Bhakta* is to give up all desires of heaven and so on. Such a heaven would be like this place, this earth, only a little better. The Christian idea of heaven is a place of intensified enjoyment. How can that be God? All this desire to go to heaven is a desire for enjoyment. This has to be given up. The love of the *Bhakta* must be absolutely pure and unselfish, seeking nothing for itself either here or hereafter.

"Giving up the desire of pleasure and pain, gain or loss, worship God day and night; not a moment is to be lost in vain."

"Giving up all other thoughts, the whole mind day and night worships God. Thus being worshipped day and night, He reveals Himself and makes His worshippers feel him."

THURSDAY, *August* 1*st*.

The real *Guru* is the one through whom we have our spiritual descent. He is the channel through which the spiritual current flows to us; the link which joins us to the whole spiritual world. Too much faith in personality has a tendency to produce weakness and idolatry, but intense love for the *Guru* makes rapid growth possible, he connects us with the internal *Guru*. Adore your *Guru* if there be real truth in him; that *Guru-bhakti* (devotion to the teacher) will quickly lead you to the highest.

Sri Râmakrishna's purity was that of a baby. He never touched money in his life and lust was absolutely annihilated in him. Do not go to great religious teachers to learn physical science, their whole energy has gone to the spiritual. In Sri Râmakrishna Paramahamsa the man was all dead and only God remained; he actually could not see sin, he was literally "of purer eyes than to behold iniquity." The purity of these few *paramahamsas* is all that holds the world together. If they should all die out and leave it, the world would go to pieces. They do good by simply being, and they know it not; they just are.

* * * *

Books suggest the inner light and the method of bringing that out, but we can only understand them when we have earned the knowledge ourselves. When the inner light has flashed for you, let the books go, and look only within. You have in you all and a thousand times more than is in all the books. Never lose faith in yourself, you can do anything in this universe. Never weaken, all power is yours.

If religion and life depend upon books or upon the existence of any prophet whatsoever, then perish all religion and books! Religion is in us. No books or teachers can do more than help us to find it, and even without them we can get all truth within. Yet have gratitude to books and teachers without bondage to them; and worship your *Guru* as God, but do not obey him blindly; love him all you will, but think for yourself. No blind belief can save you, work out your own salvation. Have only one idea of God,—that He is an eternal help.

Freedom and highest love must go together, then neither can become a bondage. We can give nothing to God ; He gives all to us. He is the *Guru* of *gurus*. Then we find that He is the " Soul of our souls", our very Self. No wonder we love Him, He is the Soul of our souls ; whom or what else can we love ? We want to be the "steady flame, burning without heat and without smoke." To whom can you do good, when you see only God ? You cannot do good to God. All doubt goes, all is "sameness." If you do good at all, you do it to yourself ; feel that the receiver is the higher one. You serve the other because you are lower then he, not because he is low and you are high. Give as the rose gives perfume, because it is its own nature, utterly unconscious of giving.

The great Hiudu reformer, Râjah Ram Mohan Roy, was a wonderful example of this unselfish work. He devoted his whole life to helping India. It was he who stopped the burning of widows. It is usually believed that this reform was due entirely to the English ; but it was Râjah Ram Mohan Roy who started the agitation against the custom and succeeded in obtaining the support of the Government in suppressing it. Until he began the movement, the English had done nothing. He also founded the important religious Society called the *Brahmo-Samâj*, and subscribed $ 100,000 to found a university. He then stepped out and told them to go ahead without him. He cared nothing for fame or for results to himself.

THURSDAY AFTERNOON.

There are endless series of manifestations, like "merry-go-rounds", in which the souls ride, so to speak. The series are eternal ; individual souls get out, but the events repeat themselves eternally and that is how one's past and future can be read, because all is really present. When the soul is in a certain chain, it has to go through the experiences of that chain. From one series souls go to other series ; from some series they escape forever by realizing that they are *Brahman*. By getting hold of one prominent event in a chain and holding on to it, the whole chain can be dragged in and read. This power is easily acquired, but it is of no real value and to practise it takes just so much from our spiritual forces. Go not after these things, worship God.

FRIDAY, *August 2nd.*

Nishta (devotion to one Ideal) is the beginning of realization. Take the honey out of all flowers : sit and be friendly with all, pay reverence to all, say to all, "Yes brother, yes brother," but keep firm in your own way. A higher stage is actually to take the position of the other. If I am all, why can I not really and actively sympathize with my brother and see with his eyes? While I am weak, I must stick to one course (*nishta*), but when I am strong, I can feel with every other and perfectly sympathize with his ideas.

The old idea was "develop one idea at the expense of all the rest." The modern way is "harmonious development." A third way is to "develop the mind and control it," then put it where you will; the result will come quickly. This is developing yourself in the truest way. Learn concentration and use it in any direction. Thus you lose nothing. He who gets the whole must have the parts too. Dualism is included in Advaitism (monism).

"I first saw him and he saw me,

"There was a flash of eye from me to him and from him to me."

This went on until the two souls became so closely united that they actually became one.

* * * *

There are two kinds *Samâdhi*,—I concentrate on myself, then I concentrate, and there is a unity of subject and object.

You must be able to sympathize fully with each particular, then at once to jump back to the highest monism. After having perfected yourself, you limit yourself voluntarily. Take the whole power into each action. Be able to become a dualist for the time being and forget *Advaita*, yet be able to take it up again at will.

* * * *

Cause and effect is all *Mâyâ*, and we shall grow to understand that all we see is as disconnected as the child's fairy tales now seem to us. There is really no such thing as cause and effect and we shall come to know it. Then if you can, lower your intellect to let any allegory pass through your mind without questioning about connection. Develop love of imagery and beautiful poetry and then enjoy all mythologies as poetry. Come not to mythology with ideas of history and reasoning. Let it flow as a current through your mind, let it be whirled as a candle before your eyes, without asking who holds the candle, and you will get the circle ; the residuum of truth will remain in your mind.

The writers of all mythologies wrote in symbols of what they saw and heard, they painted flowing pictures. Do not try to pick out the themes and so destroy the pictures ; take them as they are and let them act on you. Judge them only by the effect and get the good out of them.

* * * *

Your own will is all that answers prayer, only it appears under the guise of different religious conceptions to each mind. We may call it Buddha, Jesus, Krishna, Jehovah, Allah, Agnid but it is only the Self, the "I."

*   *   *   *

Concepts grow, but there is no historical value in the allegories which present them Moses' visions are more likely to be wrong than ours are, because we have more knowledge and are less likely to be deceived by illusions.

Books are useless to us until our own book opens, then all other books are good so far as they confirm our book. It is the strong that understands strength, it is the elephant that understands the lion, not the rat. How can we understand Jesus until we are his equals? It is all in the dream to feed five thousand with two loaves, or to feed two with five loaves;

neither is real and neither affects the other. Only grandeur appreciates grandeur, only God realizes God. The dream is only the dreamer, it has no other basis. It is not one thing and the dreamer another. The keynote running through the music is "I am He," "I am He," all other notes are but variations and do not affect the real theme. We are the living books and books are but the words we have spoken. Everything is the living God, the living Christ; see it as such. Read man, he is the living poem. We are the light that illumines all the Bibles and Christs and Buddhas that ever were. Without that, these would be dead for us, not living.

Stand on your own self.

The dead body resents nothing; let us make our bodies dead and cease to identify ourselves with them.

SATURDAY, *August 3rd.*

Individuals who are to get freedom in this

life have to live thousands of years in one lifetime. They have to be ahead of their times, but the masses can only crawl. Thus we have Christs and Buddhas.

* * * *

There was once a Hindu queen, who so much desired that all her children should attain freedom in this life that she herself took all the care of them ; and as she rocked them to sleep, she sang always the one song to them,—"*Tat tvam asi, Tat tvam asi*" ("That thou art, That thou art.") Three of them became *Sanyâsins*, but the fourth was taken away to be brought up elsewhere to become a king. As he was leaving home, the mother gave him a piece of paper which he was to read when he grew to manhood. On that piece of paper was written, "God alone is true. All else is false. The soul never kills or is killed. Live alone or in the company of holy ones." When the young prince read this, he too at once renounced the world and became a *Sanyâsin.*

Give up, renounce the world. Now, we are like dogs strayed into a kitchen and eating a piece of meat, looking round in fear lest at any moment some one may come and drive them out. Instead of that be a king and know you own the world. This never comes until you give it up and it ceases to bind. Give up mentally, if you do not physically. Give up from the heart of your hearts. Have *Vairâgyam* (renunciation). This is the real sacrifice, and without it, it is impossible to attain spirituality. Do not desire, for what you desire you get and with it comes terrible bondage. It is nothing but bringing "noses on us,"* as in the

* A poor man was once able to propitiate a certain God who gave him three boons to ask along with three throws of dice. The happy man went home and communicated the news of this good luck to his wife who, full of joy, at once told him to cast for wealth first. To this the man

case of the man who had three boons to ask. We never get freedom until we are self

---

said " We both have very ugly little noses, for which people laugh at us. Let us first cast for beautiful acquiline noses. Wealth cannot remove the deformity of our persons. " But the wife was for the wealth first and so she caught hold of his hand to prevent him from throwing the dice. The man hastily snatched his hand away and at once threw the dice, exclaiming " Let us both have beautiful noses and nothing but noses." All at once both their bodies were covered over with many beautiful noses, but they proved such a great nuisance to them that both of them agreed to throw for the second time asking for their removal. It was done, and also they lost their own little ones by that, and left completely noseless. Two boons thus they had lost and in utter dismay they did not know what to do. There was only one boon more to ask. Having lost their noses they looked more ugly than before. They could not even dream of going out in that plight. They wanted to have two beautiful noses, but they feared to be questioned about their transformation lest they should be regarded by all to be two big fools who could not mend their circumstances even with the help of three boons. So both of them agreed to get back their ugly little noses and the dice were accordingly cast. This story illustrates the previous sentence " Do not desire ; for what you desire you get and with it comes terrible bondage."

contained. "Self is the Saviour of self, none else."

Learn to feel yourself in other bodies, to know that we are all one. Throw all other, nonsense to the winds. Spit out your actions, good or bad, and never think of them again. What is done is done. Throw off superstition. Have no weakness even in the face of death. Do not repent, do not brood over past deeds, and do not remember your good deeds ; be *âzâd* (free). The weak, the fearful, the ignorant will never reach *Atman*. You cannot undo, the effect must come, face it, but be careful never to do the same thing again. Give up the burden of all deeds to the Lord ; give all, both good and bad. Do not keep the good and give only the bad. God helps those who do *not* help themselves.

* * * *

"Drinking the cup of desire, the world

becomes mad." Day and night never come together, so desire and the Lord can never come together. Give up desire.

* * * *

There is a vast difference between saying "food, food" and eating it, between saying "water, water" and drinking it. So by merely repeating the word "God, God" we cannot hope to attain realization. We must strive and practise.

Only by the wave falling back into the sea can it become unlimited, never as a wave can it be so. Then after it has become the sea, it can become the wave again and as big a one as it pleases. Break the identification of yourself with the current and know that you are free.

True philosophy is the systematizing of certain perceptions. Intellect ends where religion begins. Inspiration is much higher than reason, but it must not contradict it. Reason is the rough tool to do the hard work; inspiration is the bright light which shows us all truth. The will to do a thing is not necessarily inspiration.

* * * *

Progression in *Mâyâ* is a circle that brings you back to the starting point; but you start ignorant and come to the end with all knowledge. Worship of God, worship of the holy ones, concentration and meditation, and unselfish work, these are the ways of breaking away from *Mâyâ's* net; but we must first have the strong desire to get free. The flash of light that will illumine the darkness for us, is in us; it is the knowledge that is our nature, (there is no "birthright," we were never born). All that we have to do is to drive away the clouds that cover it.

Give up all desire for enjoyment in earth or heaven. Control the organs of the senses and control the mind. Bear every misery without even knowing that you are miserable. Think of nothing but liberation. Have faith in *Guru*, in his teachings, and in the surety that you can get free. Say " *Soham, Soham* " whatever comes. Tell yourself this even in eating, walking, suffering; tell the mind this incessantly,—that what we see never existed,—that there is only " I". Flash,—the dream will break! Think day and night, this universe is zero, only God is. Have intense desire to get free.

All relatives and friends are but " old dry wells"; we fall into them and get dreams of duty and bondage, and there is no end. Do not create illusion by helping anyone. It is like a banyan tree, that spreads on and on. If you are a dualist, you are a fool to try to help God. If you are a monist, you know that you are God; where find duty? You have no duty to husband, child, friend. Take things as they come, lie still and when your body floats, go ; rise with the rising tide, fall with the falling tide. Let the body die ; this idea of body is but a worn-out fable. " Be still and know that I am God."

The present is the only existence. There is no past or future even in thought, because to think it you have to make it the present. Give up everything and let it float where it will. This world is all a delusion, do not let it fool you again. You have known it for what it is not, now know it for what it is. If the body is dragged anywhere, let it go ; do not care where the body is. This tyrannical idea of duty is a terrible poison and is destroying the world.

Do not wait to have a harp and rest by and by ; why not take a harp and begin here? Why wait for heaven ? Make it here. In heaven there is no marrying or giving in marriage ; why not begin at once and have none here? The yellow robe of the *Sanyasin* is the sign of the free. Give up the beggar's dress of the world; wear the flag of freedom, the ochre robe.

SUNDAY, *August 4th.*

"Whom the ignorant worship, Him I preach unto thee."

This one and only God is the "knownest" of the known. He is the one thing we see everywhere. All know their own self, all know "I am", even animals. All we know is the projection of the Self. Teach this to the children, they can grasp it. Every religion has worshipped the Self, even though unconsciously, because there is nothing else.

This indecent clinging to life as we know it here, is the source of all evil. It causes all this cheating and stealing. It makes money a god and all vices and fears ensue. Value nothing material and do not cling to it. If you cling to nothing, not even life, then there is no fear. "He goes from death to death who sees many in this world." There can be no physical death for us and no mental death, when we see that all is one. All bodies are mine, so even body is eternal, because the tree, the animal, the sun, the moon, the universe itself is my body; then how can it die? Every mind, every thought is mine, then how can death come? The Self is never born and never dies. When we realize this, all doubts vanish. "I am, I know, I love," these can never be doubted. There is no hunger, for all that is eaten is eaten by me. If a hair falls out, we do not think we die; so if one body dies, it is but a hair falling.

* * * *

The superconscious is God, is beyond speech, beyond thought, beyond consciousness........ There are three states,—brutality (*tamas*), humanity (*rajas*), and divinity (*sattva*). Those attaining the highest state simply *are*. Duty dies there; they only love and as a magnet draw others to them. This is freedom. No more you do moral acts, but whatever you do is moral. The *Brahmavit* (knower of God) is higher than all gods. The angels came to worship Jesus when he had conquered delusion and had said "Get thee behind me Satan." None can help a *Brahmavit*, the universe itself bows down before him. His every desire is fulfilled, his spirit purifies others; therefore worship the *Brahmavit* if you wish to attain the highest. When we have the three great "gifts of God," a human body, intense desire to be free and the help of a great soul to show us the way, then liberation is certain for us. *Mukti* is ours.

* * * *

Death of the body forever is *Nirvâna*. It is the negative side and says "I am not this, nor this, nor this." Vedânta takes the further step and asserts the positive side,—*mukti* or freedom. "I am Existence absolute, Knowledge absolute, Bliss absolute, I am He", this is Vedânta, the capstone of the perfect arch.

The great majority of the adherents of Northern Buddhism believe in *mukti* and are really Vedântists. Only the Ceylonese accept *Nirvâna* as annihilation.

No belief or disbelief can kill the "I." That which comes with belief and goes with disbelief is only a delusion. Nothing touches the *Atman*. "I salute my own Self." "Self-illuminated, I salute myself, I am *Brahman*." The body is a dark room ; when we enter it, it becomes illuminated, it becomes alive. Nothing can ever affect the illumination ; it cannot be destroyed. It may be covered, but never destroyed.

* * * *

At the present time God should be worshipped as "Mother", the Infinite Energy. This will lead to purity, and tremendous energy will come here in America. Here no temples weigh us down, no one suffers as they do in poorer countries. Woman has suffered for æons, and that has given her infinite patience and infinite perseverance. She holds on to an idea. It is this which makes her the support of even superstitious religions and of the priests in every land, and it is this that will free her. We have to become Vedantists and live this grand thought; the masses must get it, and only in free America can this be done. In India these ideas were brought out by individuals, like Buddha, Sankara, and others, but the masses did not retain them. The new cycle must see the masses living Vedânta and this will have to come through women.

Keep the beloved, beautiful Mother in the heart of your hearts with all care.

"Throw out everything but the tongue, keep that to say 'Mother, Mother!'"

"Let no evil counsellors enter; let you and me, my heart, alone see Mother." . . .

"Thou art beyond all that lives!
"My Moon of life, my Soul of soul!"

SUNDAY AFTERNOON.

Mind is an instrument in the hand of *Atman*, just as body is an instrument in the hand of mind. Matter is motion outside, mind is motion inside. All change begins and ends in time. If the *Atman* is unchangeable, It must be perfect; if perfect, it must be infinite; and if It be infinite, It must be only One; there cannot be two infinities. So the *Atman*, the Self can be only One. Though It seems to be various, It is really only One. If a man were to go toward the sun, at every step he would see a different sun, and yet it would be the same sun after all.

Asti, "isness," is the basis of all unity and just as soon as the basis is found, perfection ensues. If all color could be resolved into one color, painting would cease. The perfect oneness is rest; we refer all manifestations to one Being. Taoists, Confucianists, Buddhists, Hindus, Jews, Mahommedans, Christians and Zoroastrians, all preached the golden rule and in almost the same words; but only the Hindus have given the *rationale*, because they saw the reason: Man must love others because those others are himself. There is but One.

Of all the great religious teachers the world has known only Laotze, Buddha and Jesus transcended the golden rule and said, "Do good to your enemies," "Love them that hate you."

Principles exist; we do not create them, we only discover them...Religion consists solely in realization. Doctrines are methods, not religion. All the different religions are but applications of the one religion adapted to suit the requirements of different nations. Theories only lead to fighting; thus the Name of God that ought to bring peace has been the cause of half the bloodshed of the world. Go to the direct source. Ask God what He is. Unless He answers, He is not; but every religion teaches that He does answer.

Have something to say for yourself, else how can you have any idea of what others have said? Do not cling to old superstitions be ever ready for new truths. "Fools are they who would drink brackish water from a well that their forefathers have digged and would not drink pure water from a well that others have digged." Until we realize God for ourselves we can know nothing about Him. Each man is perfect by his nature ; prophets have manifested this perfection, but it is potential in us. How can we understand that Moses saw God unless we too see Him ? If God ever came to anyone He will come to me. I will go to God direct ; let Him talk to me. I cannot take belief as a basis, that is atheism and blasphemy. If God spake to a man in the deserts of Arabia two thousand years ago, He can also speak to me to-day, else how can I know that He has not died ? Come to God any way you can ; only come. But in coming do not push anyone down.

The knowing ones must have pity on the ignorant. One who knows is willing to give up his body even for an ant, because he knows that the body is nothing.

MONDAY, *August 5th.*

The question is : Is it necessary to pass

through all the lower stages to reach the highest or can a plunge be taken at once? The modern American boy takes twenty-five years to attain that which his forefathers took hundreds of years to do. The Hindu gets in twenty years to the height reached in eight thousand years by his ancestors. On the physical side, the embryo goes from the amœba to man in the womb. These are the teachings of modern science. Vedânta goes further and tells us that we not only have to live the life of all past humanity, but also the future life of all humanity. The man who does the first is the educated man, the second is the *jivan-mukta*, forever free.

Time is merely the measure of our thoughts, and thought being inconceivably swift, there is no limit to the speed with which we can live the life ahead. So it cannot be stated how long it would take to live all future life. It might be in a second, or it might take fifty lifetimes. It depends on the intensity of the desire. The teaching must therefore be modified according to the needs of the taught. The consuming fire is ready for all, even water and chunks of ice quickly consume. Fire a mass of bird-shot, one at least will strike; give a man a whole museum of truths, he will at once take what is suited to him. Past lives have moulded our tendencies, give to the taught in accordance with his tendency. Intellectual, mystical, devotional, practical, make one the basis, but teach the others with it. Intellect must be balanced with love, the mystical nature with reason, while practice must form part of every method. Take every one where he stands and push him forward. Religious teaching must always be constructive, not destructive.

Each tendency shows the life-work of the past, the line or radius along which that man must move. All radii lead to the centre. Never even attempt to disturb anyone's tendencies, to do that puts back both teacher and taught. When you teach *Jnânam*, you must become a *Jnâni* and stand mentally exactly where the taught stands. Similarly in every other *Yoga*. Develop every faculty as if it were the only one possessed, this is the true secret of so-called harmonious development. That is, get extensity with intensity, but not at its expense. We are infinite. There is no limitation in us, we can be as intense as the most devoted Mahommedan and as broad as the most roaring atheist.

The way to do this is not to put the mind on any one subject, but to develop and control the mind itself; then you can turn it on any side you choose. Thus you keep the intensity and extensity. Feel *Jnânam* as if it were all there was, then do the same with *Bhakti*, with *Râja*, with *Karma*. Give up the waves and go to the ocean, then you can have the waves as you please. Control the "lake" of your own mind, else you cannot understand the lake of another's mind.

The true teacher is one who can throw his whole force into the tendency of the taught. Without real sympathy we can never teach well. Give up the notion that man is a responsible being, only the perfect man is responsible. The ignorant have drunk deep of the cup of delusion and are not sane. You, who *know*, must have infinite patience with these. Have nothing but love for them and find out the disease that has made them see the world in a wrong light, then help them to cure it and see aright. Remember always that only the free have free will; all the rest are in bondage and are not responsible for what they do. Will as will is bound. The water when melting on the top of the Himâlayas is free, but becoming the river, it is bound by the banks; yet the original impetus carries it to the sea and it regains its freedom. The first is the "fall of man," the second is the "resurrection." Not one atom can rest until it finds its freedom.

Some imaginations help to break the bondage of the rest. The whole universe is imagination, but one set of imaginations will cure another set. Those which tell us that there is sin and sorrow and death in the world are terrible; but the other set which says ever "I am holy, there is God, there is no pain," these are good and help to break the bondage of the others. The highest imagination that can break all the links of the chain, is that of personal God.

"*Om tat sat*" is the only thing beyond *Mâyâ*, but God exists eternally. As long as Niagara Falls exists, the rainbow will exist; but the water continually flows away. The falls are the universe and the rainbow is personal God, and both are eternal. While the universe exists, God must exist. God creates the universe and the universe creates God and both are eternal. *Mâyâ* is neither existence nor non-existence. Both Niagara Falls and the rainbow are the eternal changeable, *Brahman* seen through *Mâyâ*. Persians and Christians split *Mâyâ* into two and call the good half "God" and the bad half the "devil." Vedânta takes *Mâyâ* as a whole and recognizes a unity beyond it,—*Brahman*.

*   *   *   *

Mahommed found that Christianity was straying out from the Semitic fold and his teachings were to show what Christianity ought to be as a Semitic religion, that it should hold to one God. The Aryan idea that "I and my Father are one" disgusted and terrified him. In reality the conception of the Trinity was a great advance over the dualistic idea of Jehovah, who was forever separate from man. The theory of incarnation is the first link in the chain of ideas leading to the recognition of the oneness of God and man. God appearing first in one human form, then re-appearing at different times in other human forms is at last recognized as being in every human form, or in all men. Monistic is the highest stage, monotheistic is a lower stage. Imagination will lead you to the highest even more rapidly and easily than reasoning.

Let a few stand out and live for God alone and save religion for the world. Do not pretend to be like Janaka when you are only the "progenitor" of delusions. (The name Janaka means "progenitor" and belonged to a king who, although he still held his kingdom for the sake of his people, had given up everything mentally). Be honest and say, "I see the ideal but I cannot yet approach it" ; but do not pretend to give up when you do not. If you give up, stand fast. If a hundred fall in the fight, seize the flag and carry it on. God is true for all that, no matter who fails. Let him who falls hand on the flag to another to carry on ; it can never fall.

When I am washed and clean why shall impurity be added on to me? Seek first the kingdom of Heaven and let everything else go. Do not want anything "added unto you" ; be only glad to get rid of it. Give up and know that success will follow, even if you never see it. Jesus left twelve fishermen and yet those few blew up the Roman Empire.

Sacrifice on God's altar earth's purest and best. He who struggles is better than he who never attempts. Even to look on one who has given up has a purifying effect.

Stand up for God; let the world go. Have no compromise. Give up the world, then alone you are loosened from the body. When it dies, you are *âzâd*, free. Be free. Death alone can never free us. Freedom must be attained by our own efforts during life; then, when the body falls, there will be no re-birth for the free.

Truth is to be judged by truth and by nothing else. Doing good is no test of truth; the Sun needs no torch by which to see it. Even if truth destroys the whole universe, still it is truth; stand by it.

Practising the concrete forms of religion is easy and attracts the masses; but really there is nothing in the external.

"As the spider throws her web out of herself and draws it in, even so this universe is thrown out and drawn in by God."

* * * *

Tuesday, *August 6th.*

Without the "I" there can be no "you" outside. From this some philosophers came to the conclusion that the external world did not exist save in the subject; that the "you" existed only in the "I." Others have argued that the "I" can only be known through the "you" and with equal logic. These two views are partial truths each wrong in part and each right in part. Thought is as much material and as much in nature as body is. Both matter and mind exist in a third, a unity which divides itself into the two. This unity is the *Atman*, the real Self.

There is being, "x" which is manifesting itself as both mind and matter. Its movements in the seen are along certain fixed lines called law. As a unity, it is free; as many, it is bound by law. Still, with all this bondage, an idea of freedom is ever present and this is *nivritti* or the "dragging from attachment." The materializing forces which through desire lead us to take an active part in worldly affairs are called *pravritti*.

That action is moral which frees us from the bondage of matter and *vice versa*. This world appears infinite because everything is in a circle; it returns to whence it came. The circle meets, so there is no rest or peace here in any place. We must get out. *Mukti* is the one end to be attained.

* * * *

Evil changes in form, but remains the same in quality. In ancient times force ruled, to-day it is cunning. Misery in India is not so bad as in America, because the poor man here sees the greater contrast to his own bad condition.

Good and evil are inextricably combined, and one cannot be had without the other. The sum total of energy in this universe is like a lake, every wave inevitably leads to a corresponding depression. The sum total is absolutely the same, so to make one man happy is to make another unhappy. External happiness is material and the supply is fixed; so that not one grain can be had by one person without taking from another. Only bliss beyond the material world can be had without loss to any. Material happiness is but a transformation of material sorrow.

Those who are born in the wave and keep in it, do not see the depression and what is there. Never think you can make the world better and happier. The bullock in the oil mill never reaches the wisp of hay tied in front of him, he only grinds out the oil. So we chase the will-o'-the-wisp of happiness that always eludes us and we only grind Nature's mill, then die merely to begin again. If we could get rid of evil, we should never catch a glimpse of anything higher; we would be satisfied and never struggle to get free. When man finds that all search for happiness in matter is nonsense, then religion begins. All human knowledge is but part of religion.

In the human body the balance between good and evil is so even that there is a chance for man to wish to free himself from both.

The free never became bound; to ask how he did, is an illogical question. Where no bondage is, there is no cause and effect. "I became a fox in a dream and a dog chased me." Now how can I ask why the dog chased me? The fox was a part of the dream and the dog followed as a matter of course; but both belong to the dream and have no existence outside. Science and religion are both attempts to help us out of the bondage; only religion is the more ancient and we have the superstition that it is the more holy. In a way it is, because it makes morality a vital point and science does not.

"Blessed are the pure in heart, for they shall see God." This sentence alone would save mankind, if all books and prophets were lost. This purity of heart will bring the vision of God. It is the theme of the whole music of this universe. In purity is no bondage. Remove the veils of ignorance by purity, then we manifest ourselves as we really are and know that we were never in bondage. The seeing of many is the great sin of all the world. See all as Self and love all; let all idea of separateness go.

* * * *

The diabolical man is a part of my body as a wound or a burn is. We have to nurse it and get it better; so continually nurse and help the diabolical man until he "heals" and is once more happy and healthy.

While we think on the relative plane, we have the right to believe that as bodies we can be hurt by relative things and equally that we can be helped by them. This idea of help, abstracted, is what we call God. The sum total of all ideas of help is God.

God is the abstract compound of all that is merciful and good and helpful ; that should be the sole idea. As *Atman* we have no body, so to say " I am God and poison does not hurt me" is an absurdity. While there is a body and we see it, we have not realized God. Can the little whirlpool remain after the river vanishes ? Cry for help and you will get it, and at last you will find that the one crying for help has vanished and so has the Helper, and the play is over ; only the Self remains.

This once done, come back and play as you will. This body can then do no evil, because it is not until the evil forces are all burned out that liberation comes. All dross has been burned out and there remains "flame without heat and without smoke."

The past momentum carries on the body, but it can only do good, because the bad was all gone before freedom came. The dying thief on the cross reaped the effects of his past actions. He had been a *Yogi* and had slipped; then he had to be born again; again he slipped and became a thief; but the past good he had done bore fruit, and he met Jesus in the moment when liberation could come and one word made him free.

Buddha set his greatest enemy free because he, by hating him (Buddha) so much, kept constantly thinking of him; that thought purified his mind and he became ready for freedom. Therefore think of God all the time and that will purify you.

* * * *

(This ended the beautiful lessons of our beloved Guru. The following day he left Thousand Island Park and returned to New York.)